SATAN:

His Person, Work, Place and Destiny

BY

F. C. JENNINGS

LOIZEAUX BROTHERS
Neptune, New Jersey

CONTENTS

PART I. SATAN—THE PERSON

PART II. THE DEVIL'S WORK AMONGST MEN

PART III. SATAN'S PLACE AND DESTINY

Published by Loizeaux Brothers, Inc., 1975
(*Originally published by Our Hope*)

PRINTED IN UNITED STATES OF AMERICA   ISBN 0-87213-422-9

have given, and of which I have availed in the following pages.

But the subject is also one of profound solemnity, and weighty is the responsibility attached to undertaking its elucidation. We are well aware that it is only too customary, even amongst some Christians, to greet even the mention of the name of our dread enemy with a smile; or to turn a witticism with that name as though it really meant nothing; but grant even the *possibility* of such an existence, and none but fools would treat it with levity.

Grant, again I say, the bare *possibility* of the existence of such a being of transcendent powers, himself at the head of hosts of others similarly endued; to whom we owe the loss of original innocence and its accompanying happiness; who has overcome man in fair fight, even when not weighted, as now, with a corrupt nature; who is still pledged to withstand the return of every or any individual to God—grant the bare *possibility,* too, of every Christian being engaged in a conflict of life or death with such an one, and one is compelled to approach the subject—even on the assumption of these possibilities—with such awe, and so to feel the danger of either receiving or communicating any false view of it, as to cry, *"Who is sufficient for these things?"* Blessed be God, that we are permitted to add *"Our sufficiency is of God."*

I am well aware that to assume the simple existence of the Devil will be looked upon as begging

PART I.
SATAN—THE PERSON

CHAPTER I.

INTRODUCTORY.

Contents.

The subject both difficult and solemn—The divine inspiration of the Scriptures must be assumed as forming a standard of truth—What Science has to say to the subject —What Reason has to say.

———

The subject on which I desire to write is one of both peculiar difficulty and solemnity.

Of difficulty on more accounts than one, but more particularly in view of the false, and, indeed, heathenish ideas that have been bequeathed to us from times of darkness and superstition; and the acceptance of which can only be due to a guilty neglect on our part of the plain teaching of God's Word. This has indeed been largely modified of late years by many excellent works on this, and closely related subjects; and I have to express my indebtedness to these for the many suggestions they the whole question. That this, as well as all other points, must not be taken for granted, but must be proved. And this, I readily admit; only on the other hand, it must also be admitted that something must be mutually accepted as a standard of Truth to which appeal can be made for that proof.

Now, it is not within my purpose to write for those who doubt or question that those writings known as the Scriptures; or the Bible, give us exactly this standard. Were such readers as questioned this to be, at least primarily in view, it would be necessary first to seek to establish the authority of those Scriptures as providing a divine, and therefore perfect standard of truth; and however important a part this may have in Christian ministry in these days, I shall not esteem it to be necessary for those for whom I write. Yet will such a consideration of our subject—basing everything upon the Scriptures—(God giving His gracious blessing) surely result in establishing the authority of those Scriptures the more firmly where it is already held, and where there is even simple honesty and candour, it will at least be seen that they put nothing before us that is not worthy of unreserved acceptance; or that, in the dignity, reasonableness, sobriety with which they deal with this theme, give any ground for considering them other than the very Word of God. Nay, in the marvellous and beauteous light they afford on the unseen spiritual world, its inhabitants, and their connection with the Earth, and which in itself goes far reasonably to account for the contradictions and anomalies that so press upon every thoughtful mind in the things seen, they prove themselves to be as far above all human writings of all ages as the heavens are above the earth—that is, they are Divine.

Granting this, then, the next step follows as a necessary consequence, that Satan or the Devil is an actual, literal, living personality.

It is quite true that if this were put to the vote of professing Christendom at large, and that vote taken, in accord with the fast-growing democratic principles of our day, as settling or governing things, we should find that the Devil did not exist at all. We have discovered a very easy and very flattering method of disposing of disagreeable subjects. They are entirely dependent on our own will and pleasure; all we have to do is to say "we do not believe in them," or more effectually, "no one believes in them now;" or perhaps still more unanswerably, "no thoughtful person accepts them" (for we all desire to be considered "thoughtful") and lo—they are not!

Neither Judgment, nor Hell, nor Satan exist unless we choose to believe in them; and in this convenient, if thoroughly childish method, the mass of professing Christians flatter themselves that, whilst they retain all that is pleasing to them in Revelation, they have got rid of what, after all, may equally prove eternal realities, simply because these realities intrude on, and clash with, the easy-going pleasure-loving spirit of the day. It is surely the part of simple reason to learn if there be not the same clear ground for accepting one set of these as the other. Indeed, if we do accept the Bible as giving us all the light we can possibly have on such mighty facts as Christ, heaven, life; surely it is worse than folly, it is literally suicidal, to deny or ignore it as an authority on themes that are exactly of the same nature, although of a contrasted character; the Devil, hell, judgment; for in so doing, we do really—however much one may wish to avoid such a consequence—shake the very basis of all our brightest hopes.

As far as the Scriptures go, the personality of the Devil is as clearly revealed as the personality of Christ. Indeed, those who deny that of the former, really destroy the latter as a Saviour; for if He were not externally tempted to evil—i. e., if those evil suggestions to make the stone into bread, to obtain the kingdom of the earth by devil-worship, or to cast himself down from the pinnacle of the temple—did not come to Him from some living intelligence (for it is impossible to conceive of such suggestions apart from intelligence) external to Himself, then must they have come from *within;* and that being the case, He Himself needed a Saviour rather than *was one;* may God forgive even a statement of a blasphemy we repudiate and abhor with all our heart.

SATAN.

The Devil is then, according to Scripture, an actual, living, reasoning being; and, in some way, the embodiment of evil, as God of good; and who can deny it? "Oh," it is said, "such a thought even, is not in harmony with, or worthy of, the scientific attainments of our enlightened day." But what has Science to do with such a question? Science is what is *known* by human research in the various fields of natural phenomena. It has to do, from its very name and nature, with what is *knowable,* or capable of recognition in some way, by man's senses; that is, it is limited to, and has to do with ascertainable *facts,* ascertainable by man's capacities, without supernatural assistance. The very denial of there being anything beyond the limit of man's capacities is really, in the truest sense, unscientific, for it is an intrusion into that which, from its very nature, is beyond that limit and how can he assume to know anything, either *pro* or *con,* of that? For unless man's powers are infinite (in which case he is indeed God, and with such claimants argument would be thrown away) they must have a limit. If a limit, then he cannot go beyond that limit, either to deny or assert. And to claim capability for knowing what exists, or does not exist there, since this is clearly unknowable, is utterly unscientific.

It would be more strictly "scientific;" that is in accord with human knowledge and its necessary limitations, to say: "I know that since my capacities are not infinite but limited, there must be a sphere outside the limits of those capacities, as to which, from the very nature of the case, I must be dependent on external revelation coming from that sphere, if I attain to any knowledge at all." That would at least be common sense, and common sense is not very far from true science.

But this being granted, we must also admit that there may be true, and indeed unavoidable deductions drawn from evident facts, as there may also be hypotheses more or less probable based upon them; but a clear distinction must ever be made between the basal facts, and the hypotheses. The former are within the sphere of true science, the latter are outside it, and simply the progeny of a science, falsely so-called, for *hypothesis* cannot possibly be *knowledge;* yet, simple truism as this is, it is constantly overlooked. For instance, there are clear similarities, and gradations of these, in the external forms of all creatures; as, for example, there is some external similarity between the body of man and the body of the anthropoid ape; this may be called *Science,* for it is capable of proof. Evolution is the *hypothesis* based on this fact, but this is *not* science, for it remains without proofs, and the voice of protest against its claims to being this, is becoming constantly louder, and its volume is now being swelled even by scientists themselves, amongst whom there is setting in that strange, restless reaction that in itself proves how admirably selected was that word of Scripture that calls all this kind of thing *"science falsely so called."* Nothing is more misnamed than this pseudo-science to which the mass of professing Christians are bowing the knee and receiving as if it were a god. It is. A false god.

Further, it is not without deep significance that ever increasing numbers of scientific men, men with certainly no bias towards faith in the supernatural, quite the reverse, have been, and are being compelled by the utterly inexplicable phenomena of so-called spiritualism, either to predicate some new "force" with regard to whose properties and powers they are in absolute ignorance, or plainly to give that "force" the name of *"spirit."* It is true that they will admit of no spirits but those of the dead from among men, but that one need not discuss here. We know another solution to these mysterious manifestations, other spirits quite capable of producing them. The point is that when men like Sir Oliver Lodge, Sir William Crookes, A. R. Wallace, Professor Lombroso, and a host of thoughtful, careful, and, in a sense, sagacious men, who have a world-wide reputation for being "scientific," are forced, against all preconceived views, constitutional bias, educational training, and temperamental prejudices, to recognize a spiritual sphere, it is not without the greatest significance. Indeed, so far has this gone, that the method hitherto adopted of dismissal of the subject by a kind of superior

waive of the hand as being made up entirely of
fraud, quite unworthy of being even considered by
any one of discernment, is now rather an unconscious confession of superficiality and thoughtless-
ness, if not of sluggishness and cowardice, than evidence of any sincere or intelligent research, and
conviction based upon it.

But it may be further urged, apart altogether
from Science, Reason revolts at the assumption of
such an existence as the Devil. But this objection
at once provokes a counter question: "Whose reason?" It is beyond argument that, even up to the
present moment, the reason of myriads of men,
amongst whom may be counted many of the keenest human intelligence, and of profoundest human
learning, has not revolted, but has unreservedly accepted such an existence as a fact, and as account-
ing, in a reasonable way, for facts otherwise inexplicable. That the reason of a Milton or of a New-
ton, or of a Faraday did not revolt against such an
assumption is surely quite sufficient to prove that
Reason, *per se,* does not necessarily reject this clearly revealed fact.

To this of course it will be objected that those
grand intellects were themselves under the spell of
the times in which they lived; even as a Socrates accepted the false gods of heathendom from the same
cause. And it would be as reasonable to claim
from this that idolatry was as much in harmony
with reason as the existence of evil spirits. We ful-

9

ly concur, and admit that reason has never revolted at the recognition of some powers behind the idols, even the very demons of whom our subject is chief. We may say that the reason of a Socrates as of a Faraday accepted the same personality, although the one in heathen darkness and the other in the light of divine revelation, gave that personality differing names and attributes. But up to the present hour multitudes of not the least thoughtful or intelligent of mankind find nothing contrary to reason in such an existence as is so plainly revealed.

For revealed it is, and I shall not therefore esteem it necessary to go further in proving the personality of the Devil; nor would it come within the limits of my present purpose to go into the subject or even consider the striking and interesting correlative theme of demonology. Nor the closely allied one of what is called spiritualism, at least, with any detail.

I shall speak as a Christian believer, who accepts heartily and fully, and after over forty years of daily examination and search, the Bible, as a Divine revelation to men, to others of the same conviction; only seeking to get from that one pure source alone, and by the same goodness that gave it, such light as its author has seen fit to give us on the one single point of *Satan, his person, work and destiny;* and to sweep away the dust, and cob-webs of mere tradition, or popular folly that have buried this truth, obscured this light, and eventually given us a mere-

ly ridiculous parody on this, as on many other subjects, and to show that it is rather this parody that
is rejected, and that this rejection does not affect in
the slightest degree the truth of Scripture.

SATAN.

CHAPTER II.

Contents.

The most popular conception of the Devil—The possible basis for this in Scripture—First introduction in Scripture —Was the natural serpent originally evil in craft?—Was it originally as now in form?—Object of universal worship— Suggested meaning of "Dust shall be the Serpent's meat."

In considering the person of Satan, it may be well first to look at the common, vulgar, popular idea, such as is still held by the masses of Christendom, and such as is made the basis, or one of the bases, for the rejection of his very existence by many of the "learned" of the day.

The lowest possible, and yet the most widespread conception we have is in what one may term the stage idea, as we constantly see it on the posters in our streets. A human form, with leering face, characterized by a grin of low cunning, horns, hoofs, and forked tail; utterly obscene, and provoking nothing but contempt, ridicule, and disgust.

You have probably seen Albert Dürer's pictures of him: a swine-like face, a bestial body, with, of course, the inevitable horns, hoofs, and tail. It is not very surprising, since that is the popular idea, men of refinement, or learning, should have pushed the whole thing on one side, and declared him to be the mere offspring of the superstitions of the dark ages. If such a picture were given in Scripture there might indeed possibly be some excuse not only for rejecting the person, as being only worthy of those dark ages, but also the authority for such a conception.* But I hope to show that the Word of God is not responsible for a single line of such a picture as that.

Hardly had the human race been called into existence, than we find a strange enemy making his attack upon it under the guise of a *serpent.* Although the writer of this account gives no name to this creature, except "the serpent," other Scriptures leave us no doubt as to who it was. Mere serpent, mere animal, it could not possibly be; for *speech* is the distinctive characteristic of the spirit, and that this serpent possessed the faculty of speech was, and is enough to prove that some one of a higher

---

*The nearest approach to any Scriptural source for such a picture may possibly be found in a word used by Isaiah Ch. xiii:21 translated *"satyrs"* in both A. V. and R. V. ("he-goats" in mar). We may have occasion to look at this again, but the word *searim,* there used, meaning literally "hairy ones," translated also *"goats"* in Lev. iv, and yet *devils* in Lev. xvii and 2 Chron., may certainly account for the horns and hoofs of the popular picture referred to, without, however, justifying it at all.

kingdom and order than that of the beasts was pos-
sessing it.

Here, then, this strange thing of a beast speaking,
arguing, reasoning, clearly indicated that some
spirit had taken possession of it, or had assumed
the form.

But we are not left to these inevitable deductions.
Subsequent Scripture fully confirms them. The
apostle in writing to the Church in Corinth, likens
that church to Eve, and the serpent to the Devil
(2 Cor. xi), until finally and conclusively we hear
the Devil plainly called *"that old serpent"* (Rev.
xii:9)

But as thus our first introduction to the Devil in
Holy Writ is under this guise of a serpent, and as
this points to some kind of harmony between the
malign spirit and the beast whose form he assumed,
and as that reptile is held to be amongst the lowest
and most abhorred of the animal creation—ever
loathed and loathsome—so the evil spirit is assumed
to be, and ever to have been, not one of exalted dignity, but contemptible and base.

But even admitting the premises, the consequence
need not so inevitably follow. Have we not been
rather hasty in assuming that the serpent was always, from his very incipiency, exactly as we
know him now, either in nature, form, or movement?

The word for *serpent* in Hebrew (and these Hebrew words are intended to give us valuable assist-

ance in determining the nature of that to which they
are applied) is *nachash,* which may come from the
root *nachash, to hiss;* or, as Dr. Tayler Lewis
writes, "is far more likely to have had its sense
from the secondary meaning of that root—*to shine,*
whence *brass,* the *shining* metal. This gives, as the
first thought in the word for serpent, 'splendour,'
'glistening,' 'bright,' 'shining,' either from its
glossy appearance, or, more likely, from the bright
glistening of the eye. The first impressions of mankind in regard to the serpent were of the splendid
and terrible kind—beauty and awe." We shall find
this absolutely confirmed, and in a most striking
way later.

Nor does the fact that the serpent is called "more
subtle than any beast of the field" *necessarily* predicate anything essentially evil in that creature before the fall of man, or apart from diabolical possession. There are words in Hebrew that might
have been used here that would have had an unequivocally bad significance;* yet such is not used;
but *ahroom,* frequently translated *prudent* in quite
a good sense, as "a *prudent* man foreseeth the evil,
and hideth himself" (Prov. xxii:3) ; so that it may
have had, when applied to the denizen of an unfallen
creation, a distinctly good meaning. Nay, when we
remember that God *"saw everything that he had*

---

*E. g. *mismah* always translated *deceit, treachery, craft*
or *guile.*

made, and behold, it was very good"—mark *every-thing,* the serpent included—that word "subtle" must have had a good, rather than bad sense.

As we shall see, in the spiritual world the wisdom of the highest creature was admirable, but that wisdom changed to craft after his fall; so in the animal creation of earth, the serpent's original prudence became craft. The serpent that tempted Eve, being the Devil in that guise, the *subtlety* was of course unequivocally evil.

Nor would the sentence pronounced *"upon thy belly shalt thou go"* be of great significance, if this had always been the method of movement. It seems to afford some undoubted justification of the thought that many have had* of some great and radical change in the serpent's form, quite in contrast with its original glory and beauty.

In all this we see why Adam called him *Nachash.* He looked at him, discerned his qualities thoroughly, and then gave the name that expressed those qualities perfectly: "the bright, shining, splendid one," filled with a wisdom transcending all the oth-

---

*So Milton:

> "Not with indented wave
> "Prone on the ground as since; but on his rear,
> Circular base of rising folds that towered
> Fold above fold, a surging maze, his head
> Crested aloft, and carbuncle his eyes;
> With burnished neck of verdant gold erect
> Amidst his circling spires, that on the grass
> Floated reduntant: pleasing was his shape and lovely."

er beasts that he had seen. Did not then the Devil
assume his guise with consummate skill, in taking
the form before Eve that had already awakened
such considerations of admiration on the part of her
husband? Might she not safely listen to one *he*
had so named?

There is another phenomenon in connection with
the serpent that is of intense significance and profound interest in the fact that we find it as an object
of worship in all the ancient countries of the earth;
everywhere it has been recognized as a *god*. This
is a simple fact, account for it as one may. Scripture accounts for it by the fall of man from his original place of dependence upon, and confidence in,
his Creator, to placing his trust in the opposing
word of the enemy. What follows this? Naturally, reasonably, that enemy becomes, even in the likeness of that creature whose form he assumed, *the
"god of this world"* (2 Cor. iv). The sentence *"dust
shall be the serpent's* meat" may well (I do but suggest it), in that intense pregnancy of meaning that
characterizes these earliest Divine utterances, fore-
shadow this, the serpent's *portion*; the serpent's *satisfaction,* meat, or food, shall be the external worship of those whose *spirit* he has destroyed, and
who are thus well pictured by the *dust* whence they
came, and to which they return. But no worship
willingly, intelligently rendered by man's inmost being, "in *spirit and in truth,*" shall the Devil ever
have. No loving heart-felt adoration of the *soul .*

shall he ever enjoy. No, no, dust, nothing but dust, the outward prostration of the *body,* and that in horror and terror, must suffice him, and be his "food" on this earth, through all time. Let us mark thankfully the confirmation that our Lord's words give to this, even in their contrast to the Devil's meat: when, as He led one poor sinner's heart *back to God,* He said, *" I have meat to eat that ye know not of."* The Devil's meat was to get man's heart away from God, and God let him have it in a consequent external prostration to himself (as, indeed I Cor. x:20 proves): the Lord Jesus' meat is to get man's heart back to God, and a consequent willing joyful worship of Him as Father, not external, but *"in spirit and in truth;"* forever be His Name adored!

HIS DIGNITY.

CHAPTER III.

Contents.

The Devil and the Archangel—The Prince of this world —The Devil's lies are superhuman—Where is Satan's Throne—Saul a type of the Devil—Retains his kingdom of the world to this day—Other names: "Prince of the powers of the air"; "Prince of the Demons"; "God of this age."

In full harmony with all that we saw in our last chapter, we have the clearest and most explicit Scriptures for the transcendent dignity of our Subject, by his creation.

Let us look at what the Spirit of God writes by the Apostle Jude: *"likewise also these dreamers defile the flesh, despise dominion, and speak evil of dignities."* We must not pass this without a little consideration, for it throws its light on what follows.

The "dreamers" to whom reference is made are the men who have "crept in unawares" (v:4) to Christian communion; have there assumed a place of teaching, and undeterred by such examples as the deaths in the wilderness (v:5) the angels who had sinned (v:6) and Sodom and Gomorrha (v:7) still walked in the same path of assured judgment; for first *"they defile the flesh"*; secondly, they *"despise lordship or dominion";* thirdly, they *"speak evil of dignities or glories."*

In this three-fold evil may be recognized one of those references (apparently undesigned on the part of the *human* writer at least, and which thus brings out the *divine* authorship all the more clearly) to man's tripartite being, each of which carries with it the responsibilities of a certain relationship.

"Defiling the flesh" is clearly personal: affects themselves in their *bodies*. They subvert (and mark this carefully) the divinely intended order of their beings, by which the *spirit* was enthroned as ruler; this government is deposed, and their bodies are used solely for the gratification of low sensual desires of varying character.

"Despising lordships" is the same equally rebellious way in which they bear themselves to the governments of *earth,* and with which they are in relation by their *soul;* here too they subvert the divine order. Finally *"speaking evil of glories"* ascends with the same pride, into the higher sphere of the *spirit;* and the word "glories" or dignities suggests a closer connection with what is *divine.*

They, in every sphere, in every relationship, subvert God's order of government, and particularly have no reverence for those who have been divinely invested with personal dignity, or official authority; and are thus (and again carefully mark it) *above them.*

Now as a contrast—a striking contrast to these look at the highest of the elect Angels. *"Yet Michael the archangel, when contending with the devil, he disputed about the body of Moses, durst not bring against him, a railing accusation, but said "The Lord rebuke thee."* There is such a glory— such a dignity conferred on him who is here called the Devil, that even the highest of the holy angels— the only one who is ever called *archangel* in scripture—recognizing that dignity, owns that he is in some way higher even than himself, for none but the Lord can rebuke him. The rebuking implies official superiority. It is quite becoming for a superior to rebuke an inferior; a parent rebukes his children; a ruler those beneath him; an elder may rebuke one younger; but the reverse is altogether out of order and unbecoming. If the archangel then were higher than the Devil, and could thus have rebuked him, it would not have been necessary to have appealed to the Lord to do so.

The evil men of whom Jude writes had no reverence for authority higher than themselves anywhere, either in earth or heaven; whereas in contrast to these, the highest angel reverenced an official authority or glory above himself, even in one so far *morally* below him as the Devil (one must always distinguish between moral condition and official dignity); a glory of which even his present condition has not as yet deprived him.

In view of this let me ask are all these foolish and repulsive pictures; all the unworthy or slurring thoughts that we have received and harboured as to the Devil, are they consistent with truth? Do they come from God or are they pleasing to Him? Surely not; nor is it perhaps the least clear evidence of the exceeding "subtlety" of our enemy that he himself has been the author of these very falsehoods as of all others; for if he can thus bring men, and especially the Lord's people to despise him, they will be the less watchful, the less prayerful, feel less the need of being on their guard against him; of absolute dependence on the one single Arm that is stronger than his; and his control of them, quite unsuspected, will be the easier and more complete. In warfare nothing is of greater value than strategy, and well may our great enemy prove himself, in this, the greatest of strategists.

Nor do we honour Him who came *"to destroy the works of the devil,"* if we recognize His opponent to be any other, or less, than our verse in Jude proclaims him to be; *the highest of all created Intelligences!*

But to continue: in John xii:30 and again in chap. xiv:30 the Lord Jesus speaks of one as "the prince of this world,"* who can be none other than the

---

*"Not Age" in these cases.

same personage. It is not permitted us to suppose for one moment that this title gives a false, or exaggerated impression of his dignity. You and I are walking through a world, of which none other than the Son of God tells us that Satan is still its Prince. The silly parody, such as we have seen the popular conception to be, has nothing very "princely" in it surely.

The Lord does not indeed call him King, which is a title of absolute supremacy, as Peter says "the King *as supreme,*" but *"Prince,"* carrying with it, I conceive, a responsibility to recognize One still above him.

I shall seek to show later how he became Prince of this world; and why so recognized even by the Lord Jesus Himself, but the only purpose I have in referring to these Scriptures now, is to emphasize the simple fact of Satan's dignity by creation.

In further complete harmony with this, turn to Luke iv:5-6.

"And the devil, taking him up into an high mountain, showed unto him all the Kingdoms of the world in a moment of time. And the devil said unto him. All this power will I give thee, and the glory of them, for that is delivered unto me; and to whomsoever I will I give it."

Now there is nothing to show that this is a false or extravagent claim, or that he could not do as he proposes, nor does the Lord find any fault with him on this ground, nor does He answer by telling him that he has *not* the Kingdoms of the world and the glory of them; but in quite another way.

We must ever remember that the Devil never lies exactly as man does. What he does he ever does *superhumanly;* and we must be further careful to remember that because a thing is superhuman, it does not follow that it is divine, it may be Satanic, or demoniacal or angelic. There *is* a lie in the statement he made to our Lord; but it is not what we might naturally think it. It is recognized even amongst men, that, as Tennyson says,

"A lie that is half a truth, is ever the blackest of lies,
A lie that is all a lie may be met and fought with outright,
But a lie which is part a truth is a harder matter to fight."

And so the Devil so wraps his lies round with an external covering of truth that, swallowing the truth, the lie may go with it; as bitter pills are coated with sugar that they may be the more acceptable.

One more scripture gives further strength to this. In the Lord's letter to the church in Pergamos He says: *I know where thou dwellest, where Satan's* THRONE (Greek *thronos*) *is;* and this compels us to recognize first that Satan still has a throne; secondly that this throne is on earth, for Pergamos was nowhere else; and lastly that this idea of a *throne* is alone consistent with great; and, *in its sphere,* supreme dignity; although without denying a Throne outside that sphere that may still be superior.

HIS DIGNITY.

Now that he holds that position in this day by *divine right,* we may well question; but that he does hold it we must not question. You will bear in mind too, that the overruling government of God so ordered the events of earth—or at least one particular portion of it—as to cause them to picture for us similar events in the far wider sphere of the unseen and spiritual world. I do not know what words I can use to impress my readers with the importance of this, for a right apprehension of our subject. We have the most direct and clearest ground for asserting it with regard to the inspired history of Israel—*"All these things,"* says the Apostle *"happened unto them for types, and are written for our admonition, upon whom the ends of the world have come";* and he transfers from a *literal* to a *spiritual* sphere these recorded events; when, for instance, he says *"that rock was Christ."*

I therefore confidently believe that we shall find profound teaching in this divinely given history that shall be most helpful to the clear understanding of our subject.

Thus you remember that God permitted Israel to choose their first King, and they choose Saul; as to whom we are told that *"from his shoulders and upward he was higher than any of the people."* Why are we told this? Have we exhausted its significance when we picture to ourselves the towering height of that human king? I am sure not; but rather would the Spirit of God, provide a perfect figure or type of him, who, exactly in the same way, towered over *his* fellows: in other words was, as the other Scriptures we have glanced at show the most exalted of all created spiritual intelligences.

But Saul disobeys, or, to use language that shall suggest the parallel I desire to keep before us;— *"iniquity was found in him"*; see Ezek. xxviii:15; and he was set aside from his kingly office: the kingdom was rent from him (1 Sam. xv:27, 28), and then God anointed another king of His own choice: *A shepherd king,* David! Now no one questions David being a type of the beloved Son of God; why should not Saul afford us also a type of His opponent? He surely does.

But,—and this is the point that must be carefully noted and weighed,—*Saul retains the throne of Israel, and is still recognized as the king, long after he is divinely rejected;* the sentence is pronounced, but judgment is not at once executed, whilst David, the now true king, is "hunted like a partridge upon the mountains, or finds his refuge in the cave of Adullam"! God does not at once intervene by *power,* and take the dignities of the kingdom from Saul,—although he has lost all *title* to them—and put them in David's hand: the power is Saul's,— the title is David's. The latter is king *de jure,* the former *de facto.*

Do you not see the marvellous and clear analogy? Satan too, whilst he may have forfeited all *title* to the throne of the earth—we shall consider this more carefully directly—still cleaves as did Saul, to its power and dignity; claims, as did Saul, all the power of its government; whilst the true David, to whom all belongs in *title,* is as it were, in the cave of Adullam, where a few "discontented" ones, those who are not satisfied with such a condition of things—have found their way to Him, and own Him, even in the day of His rejection, as rightful Lord of all. Therefore whilst Satan is the prince of this world at the present time, we are led by the analogy of the inspired history, as by every clear Scripture, to regard Him as its *usurping* prince: a prince in *power,* but not in *title.*

Yet whilst now a usurper, as Saul was: still since he was, also as Saul, divinely anointed as king, the dignity of that anointing still lingers on him, so that Michael recognized that dignity—not speaking evil, but reverently (even as David spoke of Saul ever as "the Lord's Annointed") and saying *"the Lord* rebuke thee."

Nor are his royal dignities exhausted by the title of *"prince of this world";* he is also called *"the prince of the powers of the air",* that is, he is the recognized chief of all those spirit-beings who shared his sin, and are under him in his government of the earth, filling its atmosphere which is their natural habitation. Strange and wonder-inducing word! Are we indeed surrounded on all sides by unseen spirit personalities? Is the very air we breathe permeated and defiled with their presence? Was it due peradventure, to this, their continued presence in it, that God refrained from calling the work of that second day, "good"? Do the claims of modern spiritualists, as of ancient witchcraft, receive this degree of clear confirmation from Scripture? Yes, surely yes, to every question: little as the consequences of such an answer may be realized by us.

Again we have a parallel title to the last in "Prince of the Demons" (Matt. xii:24), assuming that Beelzebub is one of the names by which Satan was called by the Jews, as v:26 would clearly justify. He casts out demons "by Beelzebub the prince of the demons," they charged. "If Satan casts out Satan" the Lord answers: so Satan is surely the "Prince of Demons."

The word "Demon" bears with it to our ears an idea of such utter repulsiveness, such moral uncleanness as to obscure or eclipse entirely any official dignity or personal glory by creation that might still attach to one so called. But as the Devil or Satan is called both Prince of the Powers of the Air; and Prince of the Demons, and these latter are as clearly spirits (see Matt. viii:16, and Matt. xvii:18, with Mark ix:25) as the former; there would appear no good or sound reason for distinguishing between them.* We conclude that

---

*As does Pember in "Earth's earliest ages"; but his argument is not convincing.

the Demons are but the Principalities and Powers
who own Satan as Prince, only under another name;
and one which by no means carried with it at all
times its present low and repulsive idea.

But royalty is a civil dignity—a political glory—
has he no spiritual or religious dignity? Indeed,
yes, but we cannot admit *that this* is his by creation;
but rather by his own inordinate pride and presump-
tion than by any divine apportionment at all, or at
any time. In 2 Cor. iv:4 he is called "the god of
this age." In this present system of things looked
at morally and away from God, he so arranges not
merely the politics of earth, or its immoralities,
but its *religion*—for this is necessarily the force of
this title "god" as in contrast with "prince"—as to
suit his own ends.

He so weaves the course of this age: its religious forms, ceremonies, external decencies, re-
spectabilities, and conventionalities as to form a
thick veil, that entirely hides *"the glory of God in
the face of Christ Jesus,"* which consists in righteous
mercy to penitent sinners only. This veil is not
formed by evil-living, depravity, or any form of
what passes as evil amongst men; but by cold for-
mality, heartless decency, proud self-complacency,
highly esteemed external respectability, and we
must add, church-membership—all without *Christ.*
It is the most fatal of all delusions, the thickest of
all veils, and the most common. It is the way that

because it *is* religious, respectable, decent *"seems right unto a man but the end thereof is death"*; for there is no Christ, no Lamb of God, no Blood of Atonement in it.

CHAPTER IV.

"THE CHERUB THAT COVERETH."

Contents.

We have thus seen that Scripture at least is responsible for nothing contemptible, disgusting, or ridiculous in the conception it gives of the Devil: on the contrary, the picture is one calculated rather to awaken the opposite sentiments—not indeed of admiration—but of seriousness and awe as when one regards some awful scene in nature: a blasted oak, a ruined tower, a scarred mountain. But we have not yet exhausted this testimony and I must ask my readers to turn to a Scripture that must ever be of profoundest interest to any who are interested at all in our subject. I refer to Ezek. xxviii.

And even before looking at the particular passage, is not the peculiar prominence given to that single city Tyre in chapters xxvi to xxviii worthy of consideration? One single chapter (xxv) is enough to deal with the four nations; Ammon, Moab, Edom and Philistia; yet the next three chapters all refer, not even to a nation, but to one city— why this disproportion? Seventeen verses to *four nations,* eighty-three verses to *one city!* Surely Tyre is not, and never was so overwhelmingly important or prominent. Does not this at once suggest a typical or shadowy character of this earth-city; and behind it and its rulers—princes and kings—must we not see, somewhat indistinct and dim perhaps, yet sufficiently clear suggestions as to be unmistakable, of unseen spiritual verities, and these of transcendent importance? Yet whilst one may get such light as this apparent disproportion affords, we must not overlook the positive significance of this city being thus selected, and its king affording a type, and more than a type, of the dread personality we are considering.

By reading Ezek. xxvii, Tyre will be seen as *peculiarly* the *merchant* city of the earth in the Old Testament. She represents the commercial glory of the world, the wealth that accompanies it, and the *pride* that follows the wealth. The "King of Tyre" then would be an excellent figure of the "prince of this world;" source, pattern and ruler of all "the children of pride" as he is. Thus we may say, it was as *King of Tyre* he came in the temptation on the mount, showing to the Lord Jesus all the glory of the earth he claimed as his—

and it is as *King of Tyre* to-day he rules this age
of commercialism, fostering ever by it and its accompanying wealth, that pride and independence
of God that is his own path, the broad road in
which he is leading mankind to a common ruin. As
"King of Tyre" he instructs the young as to what
is "Success," and what failure; putting *wealth*
before them as alone constituting the former, and
poverty the latter. So that the man who leaves all
his wealth behind him and goes to nothing, has
made a *success* of life. He who leaves nothing, but
goes to all, a *failure!* Is not this the prevailing
teaching of our day? And it is due to *him,* the spirit
that now works in the children of disobedience.
Tyre of old had thus, too, a close and significant
spiritual connection with the Babylon of the future.
Tyre, the city "at the entry of the sea" whose
"borders were in the midst of the seas," was linked
by the ties of commerce with all the earth. All
were as Ezek., chapter xxvii, puts it, "her merchants," and all her merchants wail bitterly her fall.
So that city, seated on "many waters," Babylon the
Great, is also filled with the merchandise of the
earth, and her merchants, too, bewail her fall bitterly (Rev. xviii:11). Indeed they are very closely
connected, by commercialism, its wealth, and pride,
and it will not be surprising if we find both the King
of Tyre here, and the King of Babylon in Isaiah xiv
serving as figures of one and the same person. This
will not weaken the typical application of both

to the same one behind both, but immensely strengthen it.

There can then be no serious doubt but that we have unseen spiritual verities before us here, as chapter xxviii will be enough to prove. It opens with an address to "the *Prince* of Tyre," which, however, changes in verse 11 to the *King* of Tyre; and we at once ask is there any significance in this change; if so, what is it? We can hardly err greatly by getting our answer from Scripture.

Now there is one Scripture that makes a very clear distinction between the "prince" and the "king." In Judges vii and viii we get the details of Gideon's victory over the hosts of Midian, in which he first captures two *princes* of the Midianites, *Oreb* and *Zeeb;* but the *kings* remain at large; and he has to pursue them further; they are *Zebah* and *Zalmunna.* As far as I am aware we are quite dependent on the meaning of these names for any light on the significance of the incident, and these meanings are in every case here quite clear and indisputable, as they would need to be for satisfaction.

Oreb means "the raven"; *Zeeb,* "the wolf." Striking, is it not? for what words could express the two forms that evil ever has of "corruption" and "violence" better than these two creatures in the animal kingdom: the raven, the bird of darkness and corruption, as opposed to the dove; the wolf, the creature expressive of cruelty and fierceness, as opposed to the lamb?

34

"THE COVERING CHERUB."

Turning to the names of the kings: *Zebah* means "a slaughter made in sacrifice," exactly the same idea as in *Zeeb* the wolf, only now it is in connection with the unseen powers. So "Zalmunna" means "a *forbidden shadow,*" or *"spiritual* deathshade," a thoroughly kindred thought to that in Oreb, the bird of darkness, corruption; only again, in this case, suggesting a similar connection with the occult or spiritual powers; and as these are necessarily evil, the *kings* speak either of evil spirits, or the dual character of evil, violence and corruption, in *one* spirit. The *princes* then appear to represent evil in and governing *man;* the *kings,* that which is back of this, and dominates it, in him whom man serves as king: "the Prince (only so-called because there is still One higher than he) of this world." It is a deeper character or degree of evil, superhuman, diabolical. Oreb and Zeeb, the princes, may be simple qualities of fallen human nature; Zebah and Zalmunna, the kings, spiritual wickedness, controlling and using the merely human qualities as the king does the prince. Of course, the slaying these, is not literal, but figurative of bringing their power to nothing, by the Cross of Christ.

Throw the light of this on Ezek. xxviii and we shall see in the prince addressed in verses 1-10 a *man,* very proud, very evil, very exalted, too, but still a man; then in verse 11 the man disappears, and we shall see in the king, a spirit who is behind and above the evil man—who *can* that be? Can it be a question?

35

SATAN.

Note in the address to the *prince,* the striking similarity in that which is ascribed to him, to what is foretold of "the man of sin, the son of perdition," in 2 Thess. ii:3:

The prince of Tyre.	*The man of sin.*
Because thine heart is lifted up, and thou hast said "I am God, I sit in the seat of God."	*Who opposeth and exalteth himself above all that is called God or that is worshipped; so that he [as God] sitteth in the temple of God, showing himself that he is God.*

We may confidently conclude that the *prince* of Tyre is intended as a foreshadowing of the man of sin, in whom we also recognize the Antichrist.

Again and again, however, is the prince reminded that he is a man, and only a man—and all his pretensions are treated with keenest irony.* But when we come to the King in verse 12 there is no such word as *man* at all; all irony is dropped—the strain deepens. It is no longer simply "say," but "take up

---

*Pember in "Earth's Earliest Ages," whilst recognizing that the address to the King in v:11-19 contains "expressions which *cannot be applied to any mortal,*" yet as it would seem in direct denial of this does claim that it is the King, (as distinguished from his type the Prince), who is the great final Antichrist." Surely Antichrist is mortal.

a lamentation," a dirge, a song of sorrow† over the king of Tyre, as if God Himself were sorrowing over the ruin and wreck of His once fair but fallen creature; as we know, by His tears over Jerusalem, He ever does. Not even the king of Tyre, not even he whom he represents, shall pass to his doom without a "lamentation" from his Maker!

Let us be quite sure that this king does represent another, and to this end let us with some patience examine these few verses. Note how strikingly the address opens:

"Thou who sealest up the measure [of perfection]; *full of wisdom, and perfect in beauty."*

We must surely recognize the utter impossibility of applying such terms to any mere heathen King of a very small, and comparatively unimportant territory. This would not be hyperbole merely, but *insane* hyperbole.

This is the divine estimate and therefore a sober statement, without one single ingredient of hyperbole or irony in it. The one addressed is the highest of all creatures; indeed, he expresses creature-*perfection,* there is nothing more to be said or done. "Thou art the topstone: internally, full of wisdom; externally, perfect in beauty"; the very highest example of what omnipotence could create. How harmonious with what we have seen in Jude.

———

*Exactly the same word as used for David's lamentation over King Saul—the type of Satan—has this no bearing?

SATAN.

"Every precious stone was thy covering," i. e., God had put upon him, decked him with every form of His own beauty. Every beauty that is in the one ray of Light (God is Light), expressed by these stones, was put on him.*

"The workmanship of thy tambours and thy pipes was in thee, from the day thou wast created were they prepared."

From the very first, his complex being evidenced the beneficent intention of his Creator; it was that **he** should be *filled with joy* and find in himself every facility for expressing that joy to his Maker's praise. He needed no harp to be placed in his hand; no trumpet nor shawm; for he carried ever within himself, that which was quick to respond to the *touch* of his affections (tambours) or answer to the *breathings* of his spirit (pipes).

We must surely recognize the utter impossibility of applying such terms to any mere heathen King of a very small, and comparatively unimportant territory.

---

*Note the three recurrences of these precious stones:

12 in the High Priest's breastplate, expressive of all the display of divine beauties *in Grace.*

12 in the New Jerusalem, expressive of all the display of divine beauties in *manifested Glory.*

10 in this "King," expressive of the same beauties (only connected with responsibility: 10) in the *highest Creature.*

CHAPTER V.

"THE CHERUB THAT COVERETH" (Continued).

Contents.

———

This brings us to a sentence that is the keystone of our subject, and we must examine it carefully.

"Thou art the anointed cherub that covereth, and I had set thee so."

The word "anointed" speaks of divine appointment in the most solemn form. It was this "anointing" that was still on Saul that ever led David to speak of him with a respect amounting to reverence, as "the Lord's anointed;" and here carries with it the picture of the Lord Himself consecrating the subject of the address to the purpose for which he is by his creation fitted.

The next word that claims our careful attention, "cherub," is, according to Dr. Tayler Lewis, derived from the Hebrew root *charab,* "to cut," "to engrave"; a meaning that carries with it, like the engravings on a coin, the idea of *representation*. The cherub, we gather from the word itself, was to be the representative of God, at least in one line, as the image "cut" on a coin represents fully the sovereign, or government, that issues it. Compare Matt. xxii :20, 21.

But we are not dependent on a derivation in which there may be an element of uncertainty, to get right on the real significance of the term. Its first occurrence in Scripture will give us this, beyond any question whatever.

When our first parents had forfeited, by their disobedience, their place in Eden and were expelled *"the Lord God placed at the east of the garden of Eden cherubim and a flaming sword, which turned every way, to keep the way of the tree of life* (Gen. iii :24).

The *cherubim* here, one must gather, represent that in the character of God's government that forbade the return, or approach, or blessing of His sinning creatures. And this idea will be found quite appropriate wherever the word occurs in Scripture.

Take as a beautiful confirmation, or illustration of this the curtain and veil of the Tabernacle; both are made of blue, purple, scarlet, and fine twined linen: *cherubims of cunning work. Every color, as well as the beautiful material, speaks of some loveliness in the Lord Jesus. Do the cherubim of

---

*Not *"with"* as if the cherubim were distinct from the colors—these colors were cherubim.

cunning work accord, and add, to these? Indeed they do, for they tell us that never were those attractive beauties figured by blue, purple, or scarlet— into the meaning of which I cannot now enter—displayed at the expense of the righteousness of God. The *cherubim* were in every act of His life. If He said "Thy sins are forgiven thee," that was indeed the cloudless "blue" of divine grace, yet was it cherubic—the cherub character was there, for those very sins He took upon Himself and "bore in His Own Body on the tree." And so with every act, the "righteousness of God" was cared for.

So we may say it was the *cherub character of the veil;* that which, with divine "cunning work" was inwrought into its texture that prevented the approach of man to God, the coming out of God to man. At His death all obstacle was removed; sin was righteously put away, no longer "lay at the door," and the cherub-veil was rent in twain from top to bottom.

So, when in Ezekiel xxviii this marvellously endowed creature is called *"the cherub,"* it in itself at once suggests to us that his office was in connection with the Government or Throne of God; and further, that it was to maintain inviolate the righteousness of that Throne. In one word, we might say that the cherub was the representative of *The Righteousness of God,* and as this bears very directly on our subject, I must beg my readers to keep this in mind.

The words that follow fully confirm this: "that covereth," and as we are now at a point of crucial importance to the understanding of our subject, we will, by God's Grace, be jealously dependent on Scripture itself for our interpretations. What, then, is the significance of this word; literally,"the cherub, the covering one?" Exodus xxv:18 shall aid us to an answer. *"And thou shalt make two cherubim of gold * * * .and the cherubim shall stretch forth their wings on high,* COVERING* *the Mercy Seat.*

But what was that Mercy Seat? It was the very seat, or throne of God upon earth in that day; there God, in the glory of the Shekinah, dwelt, as it is written *"thou that dwellest [between] the cherubim, shine forth"* (Ps. lxxx:1).

Why are the cherubim *there* taking as it were that Throne under their protecting wing? It can only be, in view of what we have already seen, in order to protect that Throne from anything that might shake its foundations. But what could do that? If *"justice and judgment are the foundation."*†

---

*There are about twenty different words in Hebrew translated "cover" in our A. V.; but it is exactly the same in the original in both Exodus and Ezekiel; and (nor is this surely without intensest significance) has in it, the idea of *protection*: e. g. "thou hast *covered* my head in the day of battle" (Ps. cxl:7); and again "He shall *cover* thee with his feathers" (Ps. xcix:4).

†The word translated "habitation" has this meaning in it, as R. V. of Ps. lxxxix:14.

of His throne," then the slightest infringement of justice,—the slightest reversal of perfect righteousness of any character—whether on the side of punishment inflicted on the just, or *of mercy accorded to the guilty,* overturns the Throne—its foundations are destroyed!

From this, the covering wings of those cherubim of glory, in figure, shield it.

These cherubim then, over the ark, and of one piece with the Mercy Seat that they overshadow, again figured the Lord Jesus Christ (for everything speaks of Him in the Tabernacle) as saving the Throne of God from any taint of unrighteousness. Even in dwelling with, or entering into any relationship with sinful men—surely He alone does so.

Have you never been struck with the way the writer of the Epistle to the Hebrews speaks of these "cherubim of glory?" He adds, *"of which we cannot now speak particularly."* Is not one tempted to regret that he *could* not speak of them in the greater detail that he desired?

But does not this side-remark of the inspired writer clearly say that there was much to be said—profound meanings below the surface? Nay, do they not invite us,—encourage us—to enquire diligently as to what these may be? Have we not already found something in these *"cherubim of glory overshadowing the Mercy Seat,"* to be intensely suggestive of this most fundamental basal truth of the whole universe:

Never must mercy be exercised at the expense of righteousness, for as they were *"of one piece with the mercy seat,"* so mercy must be *of one piece with righteousness?*

We shall find this intensely valuable as speaking to us of the exalted dignity and high office of the first "cherub that covereth"—it was to protect the Throne of God.

But it may be asked, "what need was there for any *protecting cherub* in that day before sin or evil had marred God's creation anywhere? There was no danger of the Throne being affected by unrighteousness then."

If we have correctly interpreted Ezek. xxviii, we are there directly and distinctly told that he whom we now know as Satan *was* that; and our ability or inability to see any need for such an office is of no importance whatever as affecting the revealed truth.

We can, however, conceive a kingdom in perfect order, with not a breath of wrong or disorder in it, yet may it contain dignities of varying ranks, whose office it shall be to *maintain* that perfect order.

Every creature has been made with the definite end of filling some special sphere in the divine kingdom, for which he, or it, is fitted by its creation. The highest created Intelligence must have a corresponding exalted office for which he has been created; and it is difficult to conceive of any higher than that of covering the Throne of God.

Nor does that guardianship necessarily predicate

the actual presence, then and there, of disorder or rebellion or sin of any character. The possibility (nay in the divine mind, the certainty) of the entrance of evil, with all its consequences, into that unstained creation was surely foreseen, the unrivalled supremacy, the eternal stability of God's Throne must be maintained under all circumstances; and, as to the traitor Judas was given that sop that spoke of closest intimacy and affection, so the very creature who was "set" in the divine goodness, to this highest dignity in the gift of God and for which, by his wisdom superior to all creatures, he was preeminently fitted in ability to discern the slightest infraction in the divine order, the slightest infringement of righteousness—even he is the one to whom this honor is given; and yet by whom the infraction first comes.

Again, it would seem as if this office did not extend to the whole universe, but only to that sphere that was especially entrusted to the rule of Satan. This earth was his kingdom, and here must he see to it that Jehovah's supremacy is recognized. Will not the divine history of that earth again afford us an illustration of this? When God committed its government to the gentiles in the person of Nebuchadnezzar it was with the one essential and eternal proviso that he must recognize that the Most High really was above all the governments of earth (Dan. iv:17). Filled with the same proud spirit of the Devil, he ignored this, and suffered for it, till he learned, through deep humiliation, the lesson that "the heavens do rule" (Dan. iv:25, 26). Thus, to the Bright and Shining One, the Son of the Morning was entrusted the Throne of the earth, with the same proviso that he maintain the supremacy of God—he must never claim equality in this respect.

As to most of what I have written I can fall back for confirmation on the more or less commonly accepted views of well-taught Christians generally, who have been acquainted with such writings as those of Pember and others; but as to this point of Satan's primal office being to protect or cover the Throne of God, whilst, if justified, others have undoubtedly recognized it, yet I am not aware of having seen it in print, or heard it taught; my readers therefore need the more carefully to test it from Scripture for themselves.

I would note, however, that Pember, in his "Earth's Earliest Ages" notices the allusion, and at times comes very near the same conclusion. I quote:

"Anointed, doubtless means consecrated by the oil of anointing; while the cherubim appear to be the highest rank of heavenly beings, sitting nearest the Throne of God, and leading the worship of the universe (Rev. iv:9,-11; v:11-14). Possibly they are identical with the thrones of which Paul speaks in the first chapter of his epistle to the Colossians. The words 'that covereth' indicate an allusion to the cherubim that overshadowed the ark;

but we cannot, of course, define the precise nature of this office of Satan. The general idea seems to be that he directed and led the worship of his subjects."

It will be seen that I have ventured rather further than this author. Differing from him radically as to the meaning and application of the cherubim; seeing in the term quite another significance than that of "leading the worship" of any, this very difference has led me along the line of thought brought out in the text, and taken Pember in another direction. But it becomes important for us to ask, was Pember justified in saying that "leading the worship of the universe" is what Scripture gives as the office of the cherubim? He refers only to the two s. s. in Rev. iv and v to support it. But it is quite sufficient to point out that these are not called cherubim at all; but "Living ones:" *Zooa,* and have features that connect them with the Seraphim of Is. vi, but into this it is not necessary to go further here, than simply to point out that this reference is certainly not justified as *proving* the point. But apply the meaning this writer gives to any clear indisputable reference to the cherubim, and see how it will fit. For instance, whose "worship" did the cherubim at the East gate of Eden lead? Where is the idea of "leading worship" in the cherubim overshadowing and looking down on the Mercy Seat? *"He rode upon a cherub and did fly"* (Ps. xviii:10) surely has not the slightest allusion to "leading worship." But the significance of the personification of the Righteousness of God will be found in every case of profoundest and truest significance. It was apparently by this mistake, as I must conceive it to be, that Pember lost the thread that must have led him to the same conclusions as above.

To me it has been the key that has unlocked many difficulties; a light that has thrown its beam on much that before was in darkness, and given such views of the grandeur of the whole drama of the ages, of the whole scope of God's ways with men, of the beauties of the Gospel, as have again and again overwhelmed the spirit with awe and praise. But it needs the more careful testing since it lays the foundation for what we have still to consider as to the Devil's work.

But apart from this, all can see how perfectly those cherubim of glory overshadowing the Mercy Seat told out that same truth. Their faces were "toward the Mercy Seat" (Ex. xxv:20) Why? Because, looking thus downward, they saw the blood that was sprinkled upon that Mercy Seat, and in virtue of which blood alone, there is a Mercy Seat at all (Romans iii:25), and thus the cherubim were of one piece with the Mercy Seat; or, as we have said, Divine Righteousness, through the Blood, of one piece with Mercy. For all were shadows then, but they were shadows that spoke of the substance, Christ; and now woe to him who approaches the true Throne, apart from "richer Blood"; for there is one there who, as we shall see, in assumed zeal for righteousness, in assumed zeal to carry out his original commission as cherub, accuses men day and night; and none can overcome him but by the Blood of the Lamb. But in this we anticipate somewhat.

CHAPTER VI.

Contents.

But returning to Ezek. xxviii, surely no mere man
at least, be he king of Tyre or any other, could be
entrusted with so exalted an office as the protection
of the Throne of God; and if not a man, who should
it be but that highest of created spirits, he who is
now called the Devil or Satan?

The words *"I have set thee so"* are a strong re-
minder of creaturehood. "Thou didst not attain
this high dignity by thy skill or effort: I gave it
thee; thou dids't owe it altogether to Me." The
words suggest, what is elsewhere plainly told us,
the sin of this Cherub; the disowning this supremacy of God.

"Thou wast upon the holy mountain of God." It
would seem equally impossible for the words to
have any meaning in connection with a heathen king
of Tyre on earth; but, if not, are we not forced to

see some "holy mountain of God" other than Horeb, or Zion, or any other?

If my reader will turn to the following scriptures, Exod. iv :27, Ps. ii :6, iii :4, xliii :3, lxviii :15, Isaiah ii :2, xi :9, he will perceive that, in prophetic language, a mountain figures "government." Sinai is government on the principle of law. Zion is government established in grace (Heb. xii). The basal underlying idea in both is height; for as a mountain rises above the surrounding land, so does government above the people who are governed.*

The verse in Ezek. we are considering would then mean "thou hast been given a place in the very government of God, a place of highest dignity and most exalted privilege."

"Thou didst walk up and down in the midst of the stones of fire."

If our God is a consuming fire, these precious stones are, in picture, the displays of His holy sin-hating character. Even there, in perfect peace, this glorious cherub had walked in full harmony with the environment of those burning glories. The phrase "to walk up and down" carries with it the idea of living habitually; so that it is here equivalent to saying this was "thine own place," for which thou wast suited, thy *home.*

---

*Similarly J. N. D. in Syn. Vol II p. 416, "He had been also where the authority of God was exercised—on the mountain of God."

SATAN.

"Thou wast perfect in thy ways from the day that thou wast created, till unrighteousness was found in thee." Of what child of poor fallen Adam could this be said with *any* truth at all? Think, my reader. But this cherub was perfect, whole hearted in whatever he did: he filled acceptably the place in which God had set him: and of this time of Satan's existence we may have an intended illustration in the first happy days of Saul's reign, but there comes a day when there was some turning aside (as the word means) from this straight course. What that unrighteousness was we are not in this verse told; but we shall not go far before we find it.

V. 16. *"By the abundance of thy traffic,* they filled the midst of thee with violence, and thou hast sinned."*

But how could this apply to Satan? Does it possibly point to some unholy traffic, whereby other angelic creatures were seduced from their allegiance to their Creator to give their adhesion and devotion to this Cherub, thus putting *him* in the place of God? Is this the "wealth" of a proud spirit? As Absalom, also a rebel against the throne, *stole the hearts* (mark) of the men of

---

*Pember translates "by the multitude of thy *slanders.*" The root idea of the word is "to go about:" this may be, in order either to traffic, or to slander; but it has a bad significance in either case. Self is the centre. Comp. v:5 *"by traffic thou hast increased thy riches, and thy heart is lifted up because of thy riches."* Comp. too Rev. iii, *"Because thou sayest I am rich."*

"THE COVERING CHERUB."

Israel—*that* was the traffic that made *him* rich. Certainly a spirit being such as the one here pictured, would care nothing for mere material possessions; it would be folly to think it; but what the riches that men traffic for do for them, something would effect correspondingly for him. Riches give men dignity, power, superiority of position, deference; and something of this, although of quite another character than that accorded him by his creation, this Cherub by his skillful traffic gained. Nor need we eliminate entirely the idea of "slander" from the word, for it was by slandering God he subsequently gained the ear of our first parents in Eden, and this may well have been the method previously successful with the angels that followed him. And the case of Absalom, if there were any correspondence in the two rebellions, certainly confirms this, for did not *he* impugn the righteousness of the King's government in his words: *"See, thy matters are good and right; but there is no man deputed of the King to hear thee."* * * * *"Oh, that I were made Judge in the land"* * * * *"I would do him justice."* Is not this intended as a shadow of unseen things?

As the sense of power over his fellows increased, so independence, pride, the possibility of attaining even a higher place than was his, must have grown: *"and thou hast sinned"* is the divine and most solemn verdict.

SATAN.

Therefore have I cast thee as profane out of the Mount of God; and I have destroyed thee, O covering cherub, from the midst of the stones of fire.

A sentence not yet actually executed (for we find him long afterwards in heaven,) although pronounced. He, too, as all others sooner or later, must go "to his own place," which is no longer the holy mount, but that awful environment in harmony with his changed condition or character from the Stones of Fire to the Lake of Fire!

V. 17. *"Thy heart was lifted up because of thy beauty; thou hast corrupted thy wisdom by reason of thy brightness."*

Here we have a very clear and express statement as to what the iniquity was that was found in him: it was *pride, puffing up,* exactly in conformity with 1 Tim. iii:6, *"lest being lifted up with pride, he fall into the fault* (Grk. krima, Eng. crime) *of the devil."* Here was the first sin that broke the calm of eternity, and stirred up that storm that has not ceased to rage, with ever increasing violence since; and shall, till He quells it forever by His word, "Peace be still!"

But note, his *wisdom,* which was to maintain the creature-place of dependence—was "corrupted"; an element of ruin has come into his being. His "prudence" has become "craft." The very endowments of His Creator are made the basis of self-exaltation; and his wisdom is no longer that: it is corrupted. So, in restoration the first step, "the beginning of wisdom" is "the fear of the Lord," lowly self-judgment before Him; and the taking simply our own true place of having sinned.

"By reason of thy brightness;" that is, his own splendor, his own beauty occupies him, and is the cause or ground of those lofty thoughts that result in his fall.

How closely Absalom resembled him in this, too, may be seen in 2 Sam. xiv:25: *"But in all Israel there was none to be as much praised as Absalom for his beauty; from the sole of his foot even to the crown of his head was no blemish in him."* One special feature of his beauty is told us; it was his luxuriant growth of hair (verse 26). By that hair he was caught—*his beauty, too, became his destruction.* Surely such correspondences are not without any significance.

We need not follow our prophecy in Ezek. xxviii further, for now it seems to turn back again to earthly things, and the spirit-being once more recedes.

I have thus, somewhat more hurriedly than I would have liked but for the fear of overtaxing patience, run over this important Scripture. To sum up, it has given us, and I think convincingly, these points:

1st. By its setting and language it can apply to no child of fallen man—that is impossible.

2d. It must therefore necessarily refer to a spirit or angel.

3d. This angel or spirit, whoever it was, was personally the topstone of that primal creation.

4th. His office was to protect the Throne of God, to forbid the approach of evil, or any unrighteousness.

5th. Iniquity was found in him, and that inquity was self-exaltation.

6th. Sentence of expulsion from his place is pronounced, although not actually, or at least fully, executed.

CHAPTER VII.

"LUCIFER, SON OF THE MORNING."

Contents.

God did not create the Devil—Did not bear that name originally. What name did he bear? Isaiah xiv—Babylon and her spirit-dwellers shadowed by mystic creatures— King of Babylon *therefore* Prince of Demons—Lucifer— Propriety of such a name for the highest creature—The Bright and Morning Star—If the Devil did not come from God, whence did he come?—When, and why, called Devil and Satan?

But, further, we have hitherto considered the dignity that was the Devil's by reason of his office, or position, rather than that distinctly of his person; although naturally the former is so closely connected with the latter as to necessitate our looking at it as we have done. When God, in His perfect wisdom, creates a being to fill an office, it follows of necessity that he is fitted for that office by every quality with which he is endowed.

Our first introduction to the Devil on the page of holy writ is as he is now, working death to our race by his subtlety, so that we are apt to conclude, without much thought, that this has been his char-

acter from the beginning of his existence; but a
very little consideration will show this to be both
impossible and unscriptural.

God is absolute Good, and only Good. Nothing
that is not good could come from such a Source.
A sweet fountain may send forth poison: the Sun
may produce darkness and night, sooner than God
produce evil in the sense of wickedness.* He
therefore no more created the Devil as such, that is
as he now is, than He created *man* as he now is
(Ecc. vii :29). No "liar," no "murderer" ever
sprang from his creative will: and the Devil was
that from his beginning (John vii :44). But then it
follows that He could not have given the creature
that did come from His Hand any such name as
Devil or Satan; for such names would not have
expressed Him, as all divinely-given names ever do.

But if these were not, what *was* his name at the
very first? It must have had a good significance
expressive of the glories and dignities that we have
seen to characterize him then. It would have no
hint of moral evil; yet since we first see him as
bad, the reference to it would probably be connected with the recognition of some moral lapse.
Well, we have exactly such a name; one that would
beautifully and perfectly express one created in the
perfection of creature-wisdom and fitted to main-

---

*Is. xlv :7 *"I create evil:"* here evil is not the antithesis
of good, but of *peace.* It speaks of God's Hand upon
men in chastening judgment.

tain his high rank, yet who had lost it; it is in
Is. xiv, *"How art thou fallen from heaven, O
Lucifer, son of the morning."*

The prophet is apparently speaking to the King
of Babylon; yet, as in the case of the King of
Tyre in Ezekiel, the language is of such a character as to make it almost, if not quite, impossible for
us not to see a far greater than any mere human
transgressor in this Lucifer.

We know well that it is not at all uncommon in
these prophetic writings for them to begin with
a mere man; and either gradually, or suddenly, to go
behind and beyond the man to one who is far more.
How often are we looking at David, and even as
we look, David disappears; and beyond, and behind David, we find ourselves occupied with "David's Greater Son." So here, it would surely be
beyond the limits of hyperbole to say of any mere
human king: *"Thou hast said in thine heart, 'I
will ascend into heaven. I will exalt my throne
above the stars of God. I will sit upon the mount
of the congregation, in the sides of the north. I
will ascend above the heights of the clouds; I will
be like the Most High."* Such language would be
absurd and puerile through its very extravagance
in the mouth of any mere human King of Babylon, however closely he may have walked in a similar proud path; but as addressed to the *spirit* who
may have controlled that monarch—as applied to
one who had indeed "fallen from heaven," the lan-

guage is simply calmly reasonable, and filled with significance. Nor is such a view at all new. Even before the Christian era it was assumed that Satan was the one addressed; whilst Christian commentators, both ancient and modern, have contended to the same effect.

In this connection the context may well be considered. It is the Burden of, or Judicial Sentence on Babylon. She is to be completely destroyed; but further, such strange terms are used to portray her condition, such mysterious creatures dwell in her, as shall in themselves provide figures of the condition of, and spirit-dwellers in, the spiritual Babylon of the New Testament Apocalypse. *This* is to be "the hold of every foul *spirit*" and to forecast this in the literal Babylon, in a way that no clearly expressed beast in nature would do, strange and doubtful terms are used:

> "*Tziim* (literally, "desert-dwellers") shall rest there,
>
> And the houses shall be filled with *ochim* ("howling ones"),
>
> And *Benoth Yaanah* (lit. daughters of howling) shall rest there,
>
> And *Searim* (hairy ones, demons) shall dance there,
>
> And *Iim* (crying ones) shall cry in their desolate palaces,
>
> And *tannim* (monsters) in the pleasant castles."

"LUCIFER."

The word Searim translated in A. V. "Satyrs" we have already glanced at as of particular interest and value. It is literally "hairy ones," and thus becomes applied to the he-goat, as in Lev. iv; but in Lev. xvii:7 it could not mean this, and is translated "devils," as also in 2 Chron. xi:15. The Sept., too, renders it by *"vain things";* Targum *"demons."* There is thus an ambiguity that may well be designed, as intending to lead us to recognize all these strange creatures as types of the spirit-dwellers in Babylon at the end—evil spirits. Does not this serve to strengthen the thought that the King of Babylon here, whilst he too undoubtedly stands for the future human king, yet goes beyond and behind him, to Beelzebub, the prince of the fallen angels, or demons, even the fallen Lucifer of the next chapter?

But there is another confirmation of this. Who would so appropriately figure "The Prince of this World" as the head of the first and pattern-world power, Babylon? One might have said of Nebuchadnezzar, himself, that he was prince of this world; and so of each of his successors. We may, then, confidently accept him as a figure of the unseen power behind him, till, as we hear the cry *"How art thou fallen from heaven, O, Lucifer, Son of the Morning," he* disappears, and we are listening to an address to "the Cherub that Covereth" under his first true glorious name of Lucifer.

Let us, tentatively assuming the word thus rendered in our A. V. to be the name originally conferred upon him, examine it a little closer to determine its appropriateness. "Lucifer" is of Latin derivation, and means "Light-bearer"; but the original word in Hebrew "Hillel" means "Bright or Shining One." *Exactly the same meaning as* "NAHASH," *the name first given to the Serpent as originally created!* Is not this most suggestive and significant? But to this is added *"Son of the Morning,"* which is simply a Hebrew poetical form of speech for *the morning star.* So that putting the two together we are startled to find the first name given to him who is now our mighty foe was "The Bright Morning Star."

Naturally, the first feeling to Christian hearts is rather one of opposition and resentment as they remember that that is exactly the title the Lord Jesus assumes twice in the book of Revelation; the very last sweet and attractive character in which He presents Himself for His people's consideration, and which leads Spirit and Bride to say "Come"! Can that title have ever been given to another?

The head of the human race was called Adam; have you never heard of One Who, when that first head had brought death on all by his sin, under the same name of *Last Adam* brought Eternal Life to all connected with Him?

He called Himself *"The Vine";* can that title have ever been given to another? Indeed it was, for Israel was so called (Is. v.).

He called Himself *"The Witness."* Can any others have ever been called this? Indeed they have been in Isaiah xliii. Nay, we shall find that many a holy title or name, that has been placed upon, and dragged in the mire of failure by the creature, He, the Divine One, picks up, and assuming it Himself, lifts to a higher than its pristine level, makes it good in its fullest sense, and carries out its meaning. Further as, in every place, in every sphere, in every office we shall find the strongest, sharpest contrast between the highest of created intelligences, the subject of our book, and the Son of God; so in this very name there is a peculiar appropriateness. Lucifer (as I call him for convenience' sake) was, as he left the creative Hand of His maker, *"The Bright Star of the Morning";* but, alas, whilst that morning opened fair, with "morning stars singing together, and all the Sons of God shouting for joy" (Job xxxviii:7) and it may be with this "morning star" leading that grand choir, for is not his own destined kingdom coming into being?—it soon clouded over; and as far as this earth at least is concerned, he was the harbinger of a gloomy day. Blessed be God, there is another true "Bright and Morning Star" that shall usher in a day of eternal calm and brightness founded on redemption, righteousness, and holiness, and who also leads the singing of His people (Ps.xxii). But would not such a name be perfectly appropriate and filled with significance? Surely it would.

SATAN.

Some will perhaps ask, if he did not come from God, as the Devil, since God cannot produce evil, where *did* he come from, or how was he produced in that evil character? I have neither wish nor ability to go into matters too high, or too deep for plain people like myself, yet may we perhaps, even in a simple way, get some light on this problem. We have seen him presented to us in Scripture as the highest expression of creature perfection. Then let me ask, "Which is highest in the scale of creation, a tree or a stone?" You at once answer "a tree." "Why?" "Because it has more freedom in life and growth." "True. Which is highest, a tree or an ox?" "An ox." "Why?" "Because it has will and freedom of motion according to that will, which the tree lacks." "True again. Once more: which is higher, an ox or a man?" "The man." "Why?" "Again because he is not controlled—narrowed—limited by the laws that shut in the brute creation. By his spirit he is capable of recognizing his Creator; he becomes therefore a creature with a moral responsibility; but this predicates a greater *freedom of will,* and its powers of going in any direction."

Then do you not see how the highest of all creatures must, by that very fact, be launched from his Maker's hand, with no external clog of heavy flesh—a gross material body that forbids the free and full exercise of his desires—with no internal law compelling him ever to continue on certain prescribed moral lines whether good or bad; but

with liberty and power of going in any direction.
Indeed in such perfect equipoise as to leave him
truly *free*. Milton's words, applied to Adam,
might with even more justice be applied to his
predecessor, Lucifer:

> No decree of God
> Concurring to necessitate his fall,
> Or touch with lightest moment of impulse
> His free Will, to her own inclining left
> In even scale.

Thus was Lucifer created, nor was there, as in
Adam's case, any external influence or pressure or
temptation to affect him; he was in the highest
personal creature-perfection, in absolute equipoise
with no depraved nature tending to the one side,
as no actual compulsion to the other. The only
question is, will he maintain it?

The answer is in the names he bears. He fell,
and the very prophet who tells us his original
name, tells us of the loss of it, as he wails, "how
art thou fallen from heaven, O, Lucifer, Son of
the Morning?" As the Devil he is self-made.

Nor were the names Devil or Satan applied to
him at once; he could not be the Devil or Accuser
until there was someone to accuse; nor could he
be Satan or Adversary until there was someone
against whose blessing or mercy he could protest;
and we are told of none prior to man's fall; these
names must then have been given him after that
crisis.

SATAN.

Thus note the divine exactness, in this respect, of those first chapters of Genesis that the blind Learning of the day would eliminate from the inspired volume as mythical. *Had* he been called Devil or Satan there and then, the names would not have suitably expressed his character as manifested up to that time, for as yet there was no one to accuse; and this would have justified a charge against the divine inspiration of this Scripture. The omission of all names here is in perfect harmony with all revelation.

As Satan, the Opposer of blessing to guilty man, we see him in many passages of the Old Testament. Yet so apparently righteous are his pleas, so well-founded in the evident guilt of the accused, that many commentators emphatically assert that the Satan of the O. T. is really a kind of spiritual Attorney-general to prosecute evil wherever found; and in so doing he is as much a minister of God, and doing good service as any such officer on earth, for he is a minister of strict righteousness. There is unmistakable truth in this as the Scriptures themselves witness in saying that he "transforms himself into an angel of light" (2 Cor. xi:14), and whenever he does so it is always to resume the office of, or assume still to be "the Cherub that Covereth."

His full, true character is only revealed, his full true name is only told us, as are so many other things in the spiritual world, when the Lord Jesus

Christ comes in the flesh, and he attacks Him. Then for the first time is he plainly called the Devil. There in that one battle with its three-fold movement in the wilderness, on the mountain top, on the pinnacle of the temple, was one of the crises of the Eternities. Could he but have succeeded in deceiving, or turning aside, *this* Son, as he had the *first,* what would have been the consequences? God would either lose His beloved Son, or lose His Throne by unrighteousness. "Blest be the Victor's Name"—the result was never for one instant in doubt. The Devil may accuse God's poor failing people, he can never accuse their Champion; who shall eventually silence all his accusations even against those failing people so that none shall lay anything to the charge of God's elect with even a shadow of *righteousness?*

SATAN.

CHAPTER VIII.

FURTHER EVIDENCE OF CONNECTION BETWEEN THE DEVIL AND THE EARTH.

Contents.

The principle of "Thou and thy House"—The deed of the Head affects all in relationship with him—So Adam—So Noah—So in Israel—So Achan—So Dathan and Abiram —On what did the Devil's Sin have effect?

We may now seek to get more directly the relationship, or connection, between this Earth and Satan. We have seen that God did not create any one who could be, at his creation, called the Devil or Satan; that quite another name must have been applied to one fresh from the Hands of Absolute Good. But let us ask—for the analogy will help us much—when *man* fell by sin, did his fall affect no one but himself, or did it include both the sphere of his government and the race that sprang from him? Scripture gives its holy and blessed light on this intensely interesting question. Let us turn to Rom. viii: *"For the earnest expectation of the creature waiteth for the manifestation of the sons of God; for the creature was made subject to vanity, not willingly but by reason of him who hath subjected it."* That is, it was not through any exercise of its own will, but through the doings of some other, the creature became subject to vanity. When the first man, the head of this old creation, lost his place with God, all that creation of which he was the head, fell into disorder and confusion, all passed with its head under the shadow of "vanity," or the "bondage of corruption." From this we clearly gather that we do not see, in any part of that creation of which man is the head, that perfect beauty, harmony, or order that expresses the primal intent of its Creator. The antipathies that are so sadly evident everywhere, even in the vegetable kingdom, the feeding of the strong on the weak, the enmity between man and the beast, are all consequences "of man's first disobedience, and the fruit of that forbidden tree," and since they break in on God's purpose, since they do not express Him, since they tell of corruption, they must necessarily be transitory, not eternal, and the words "vanity" or "the bondage of corruption" express this. In one word, man, in his fall, dragged down the whole creation, of which he was the head, with him, although this was in itself guiltless, and without moral responsibility.

Let us strengthen our argument from analogy by another clear phenomenon in Scripture. In Israel, under its kings, the conduct of the king affected vitally every individual in his kingdom. Whenever the king walked with God, his kingdom

was in prosperity; whenever the king did evil, the
effect fell on his kingdom. David's sin in num-
bering the people, had its results, not on himself
alone, but in a pestilence that raged for three days
amongst his people; and so ever and always.

See this principle, clearly evidenced in the ways
of God with the families of men, both in the way
of salvation and punishment. Was it because of
the personal faith and piety of Noah's sons that
they were saved from the Deluge? There is not
a hint of anything of the kind, and the after-his-
tory of Ham tends strongly to disprove it. No,
it is "for *thee* have I seen righteous." And whilst
Noah's faith and piety did not take his family
into heaven it did keep them out of the waters of
the flood.

Again, on the other hand, look at the cases of
Achan, or Dathan or Abiram. See the wives and
little ones, perfectly innocent as those babes must
have been of any personal share in the sin of the
head of the family, yet they suffer from the effect
of that sin; as far as this earth went. It did not
keep them out of heaven necessarily, nor send them
into eternal perdition; but it brought them into the
same death that was its penalty on the actual sinner.

This will surely be enough to lead us to look for
some similar consequences of the fall of him who
is divinely called "the prince of this world."

In the second verse of the first chapter of

AND THIS EARTH.

Genesis, we are told that *"the earth was without form and void";* and the only question is, is that the condition in which God created it? Let our faith as to this stand, not *"in the wisdom of men, but in the power of God,"* and this can only be by letting other scriptures give us their light.

The very words in Hebrew tell out even to ears that may know nothing of this language, by their very sound their meaning. The phrase, *Tohu v'bohu* (without form and void, or waste and desolate) speaks by its very sound of a wail as of sorrow over the *lapsed* and *ruined* scene it describes, and corresponds in this with the "lamentation" over the covering cherub that we have already considered; and this is fully confirmed in their use in the only two other passages in which they are found together; in Isaiah xxxiv:11 and Jeremiah iv:23; and their clear force in these cases must govern our views of their bearing in Genesis.

In Isaiah the whole context is descriptive, not of a normal or natural state of things, not of an early stage of development, or of incipient evolution to higher things, but of utter desolation from the intervention of God in judgment: *"And he shall stretch out upon it the line of confusion* (tohu) *and the plummet of emptiness"* (bohu); that is, their desolation shall be as complete and shall be exactly measured with the line and plummet of the chaos from which the earth was recalled. It speaks thus of a *ruined* condition, not immature development; of degeneracy, not of evolution.

SATAN.

So in Jeremiah iv:23, 26: *"I beheld the earth, and it was without form and void (tohu v'bohu), and the heavens and they had no light. I beheld the mountains, and, lo! they trembled. I beheld, and, lo! the fruitful place was a wilderness, and all the cities thereof were broken down at the presence of the Lord, and by his fierce anger."* There can be no question as to all this picturing *a ruin* of what had once been whole and fair; again, degeneracy, not evolution.

Signifying thus a ruined condition wherever used, it is absolutely compulsory to take them in the same sense here; and it follows that the second verse in the Bible, does not describe a state of immature development; the very first condition of the earth, but a *ruin*.

This is well worthy of our meditation; for it lays another stone in the foundation of our building upon which much will rest, and therefore it was necessary to prove it clearly. We need next only ask a question or two that answer themselves to show its connection with our subject: Does God ever create ruins? Common sense itself would permit but one reply; and He Himself confirms the verdict of this lower court, when He says clearly and definitely: *"He created it not in vain"* or *tohu* (Is. xlv:18). Nothing ever comes in that condition from His Hand.

How then did this ruin come? Well, we have these proved facts upon which to base our answer:

AND THIS EARTH.

(a) The most exalted of all spiritual intelligences becomes the first sinner.

(b) To him was committed the government of this earth; he is prince of this world.

(c) That earth is seen, on our first introduction to it, in ruins.

In view of the scriptures that we have looked at, there would not appear the possibility of a question as to the link between these two "ruins"— the spiritual or moral, in Satan; the material in his kingdom, the earth; this is the consequence of that. Lucifer has fallen: his kingdom is waste and desolate; covered with restless, salt, barren waters; that great deep, over which dense darkness ever broods.

CHAPTER IX.

THE DEVIL'S LIMITATIONS.

Contents.

Contrary errors to be met—Has no essential attribute of deity—Not omnipotent, nor omniscient—Cannot infallibly foretell future events—Evidenced in modern spiritualism—Cannot give life nor raise from the dead—Personal appearance if manifested—Concluding lessons from this part.

But whilst we have thus by the truth of the Word of God, swept away many false views as to the personality of the Devil on the side of his dignity by creation, yet are there other errors on the other side—his limitations as a creature, that must not be overlooked.

He never was *"in the form of God."* Whatever of dignity or glory was essentially divine we may safely say was never his; nor any of those attributes confined to deity. To assume equality with God was "robbery" for him.

It is popularly supposed that he is omnipresent; that he is capable at one and the same moment, of directing an assault in America, of hurling his fiery darts with his own hand in all parts of Europe; of personally maintaining his kingdom in Asia, Africa or the islands of the sea. Every believer assumes, as did Luther, that he himself is the object of the direct personal assault of the one arch-enemy of mankind. Scripture does not so teach. When he was personally dealing with the Lord Jesus he was nowhere else; and when he "left him for a season," he did not remain with Him at all. It is true that there are hosts of evil ones; subordinate principalities and powers that do his bidding, and one may speak of these as merely the representatives of their Master with perfect truth. Swift in flight, too, beyond our conception may these spirit-essences be; but that is not omnipresence.

Aye, and with possibilities of communication of which our telephone and wireless telegraphy may give us suggestions, one can readily apprehend the powers these spirits may have of communicating with one another from one end of the earth to the other in a moment of time. Simultaneous communications may come from India, Australia, and America to some "medium" or human agent of the enemy, say in London ("cross-communications," each medium receiving a portion of the message only, so that these portions have to be pieced together to be complete, and thus making it impossible to be the result of *human* fraud)— that shall serve the purpose of him who sends them by his agents, but *that* is not omnipresence.

SATAN.

Then again he has not the divine attribute of omniscience. The language of Ps. cxxxix—*"there is not a thought in my heart but thou knowest it altogether"*—could not be used with regard to him. Superhuman skill has he to discover motives and detect the line of man's thoughts; but we are forbidden by Scripture from attributing to him the power that alone belongs to "the Word" of discerning "the thoughts and intents of the heart." That is again God's sole prerogative.

A third mark of creature limitation we must note in his inability to infallibly foretell the future. This is also an attribute of the Creator rather than of any creature, as Is. xli:23 clearly proves: *"Show the things that are to come hereafter; that we may know that ye are gods."* This power is *claimed* indeed by spirit-mediums. For in all these ways we must still remember that where men turn away from light, a double darkness is upon them; and that they thus put themselves in a peculiar way in the power of the evil one, so that the "strong delusion" of which we read in 2 Thess. ii has many a forerunner in minor, but still very striking delusions even in the present day.

In that day God shall permit him to deceive the whole world by the very evidences that made Israel say *"Jehovah, He is God, Jehovah, He is God,"* (1 Kings, xviii). Fire shall then appear to come from heaven. An image made of dead matter shall appear to have life since it apparently breathes freely (Rev. xiii). Who will be able to withstand such "proofs?"   So to-day those who have commerce with those evil spirits often have the chains of deception riveted the more tightly upon them in somewhat the same way.   They have to do with *superhuman* subtlety, *supernatural* skill and intelligence, and consequently it naturally transcends the powers of human skill to fathom the delusions. And the more men give themselves up to this unclean traffic the more the powers of evil are permitted to ensnare them. Future events are 'foretold, and whilst at times these prophecies are utterly at fault, yet at times it would appear as if God permitted their literal fulfillment, possibly even by the direct agency of the same spirit-powers that gave the prophecy.   Marvellous memory and knowledge of the details of individuals' lives do these spirits show; marvellous skill, derived both from their powers by creation, and 6,000 years of dealing with mankind, in discerning motives do they possess; and equal skill in using what they know; yet is the highest Prince of all these spirits but a creature; and of limited powers; he cannot infallibly foretell as to the future.

Over all His own, who walk dependently upon Himself the Lord throws His protecting shield. Around each one is that hedge that Satan found it impossible to pierce in Job's case, till divine love saw it good even for Job's sake to give that permission. And this is a very great mercy. No child of

God need ever be distressed by any of these mysterious phenomena that are now engaging the attention even of the leaders of mankind. Nor need he be ever perplexed by the experiences of others. That Holy Word in his hands throws its light on all; he knows well that it is not the spirits of the departed dead that communicate with mankind, but the evil spirits, or fallen heavenly powers themselves; and they often enough prove themselves "lying spirits" when they attempt to foretell events.

A fourth, and a very distinct limitation is the power to give life. This is peculiarly the gift of God, and again peculiarly His prerogative. Scientists may tell us that the infinitely varied forms of matter all come from some primordial germ, or protoplasm; but when we ask whence did life come? they are silent, and that question, we are quite bold to say, they will never answer till they bring *God* into their calculations, and then the answer will be simple. In a far-passed day two servants of our Subject, Jannes and Jambres also reached their limit, and were forced to own the Finger of God in the evident giving of life to the dust of Egypt. On the other hand our Lord Jesus "was declared to be the Son of God with power— by the resurrection of the dead."

That is, when He did raise dead people, such as Lazarus or the Widow-of-Nain's son to life, that proved Him to be the Son of God. The Devil can neither give life, nor raise from the dead. He may imitate this by causing the image of the beast to breathe; but we must not read with our A. V. that *"he had power to give life"*; but with the Revised *"it was given to him to give breath to it"* (Rev. xiii:15).

We may then be permitted to close this part of our subject by a picture of the personal appearance of Satan as justified by Scripture. Were he to be manifested in form and feature, we should see a being with marks of extraordinary pristine beauty; yet a beauty that is past, "corrupted by reason of his brightness" that is by the awful change of character due to his fall. Not in the bloated features of the drunkard, nor in the repulsive bestiality of the libertine would his loss of beauty consist. Indeed in the eye of the people of this world, the marks of his pride might not be counted a marring at all; that pride would be considered admirable as it is in "a man of spirit" to-day; the imprints of stupendous ambition might be seen as noble; the wrinkles of pitiless malice, whereby he has followed his own ends, might not be discovered as even blemishes; but to the opened eye of the saint, he would have no beauty at all. Just as, on the contrary to the world or unbelief, the Blessed One had "no beauty that we should desire Him," whilst to faith He is, and ever has been, the "altogether lovely."

Thus the men that shall head up and be the fullest expressions of evil in the earth, will not show

any of the marks that would awaken the contempt
or loathing of mankind to-day—on the contrary
they will have many of exactly the same character-
istics as the world's heroes now bear. They will be
intensely energetic; of great courage and boldness;
exceedingly clever and talented; very ambitious
and successful in life; caring nothing whom they
may destroy in attaining their ends; high-spirited
and (at least in the earlier stages of their career)
with a great assumption of, and regard for *righteousness*—all of which are regarded as admirable
qualities, but all quite possibly consistent with a total
lack of regard for the claims of the Lord Jesus
Christ, a total rejection of His atoning substitutionary work, as we well know, and consequently, all
possibly consistent with all that is Anti-Christian.

My beloved brethren let us most prayerfully watch
against the spirit of the day, which covers its unbelief and rejection of our Lord Jesus, both in the
essential integrity of His Person and His work, by
a great assumption of regard for *"righteousness."*
Fair as it all may sound, it is of that apparent angel
of light the Devil, who cares little for man's zeal
for external righteousness; nay, may instil that zeal,
if, by it, he may the more effectually attack the Son
of God.

PART II.
THE DEVIL'S WORK AMONGST MEN

CHAPTER X.

ITS ROOT CHARACTER.

Contents.

In considering what the Scriptures teach to be
specifically and directly the Devil's work amongst
men, it may be well to pursue the same course as
we did as to his Person; that is, first to look at the
popular idea; and we shall find this quite as far
astray from the truth in this case as in that. Indeed
God's Word will be found to teach the very opposite
of what is popularly held.

People are accustomed to say of such-an-one, "he
is gone, or going to the Devil." It is a careless
flippant form of speech that reveals how little those
who use it grasp the official dignity and personal
superiority by creation of him whose name they thus
lightly use. Indeed it is mostly thus spoken by those
who are least awake to his existence; but let us
take it up—it will suit our purpose—and look at the
man who has "gone to the Devil."

He is squandering, or has squandered his means
in riot and debauchery.

He has sunk, and is ever sinking lower, in the social scale. He has long lost all self-respect, and the respect of others. His friends of past years have, one by one, dropped him; till perhaps, a faithful yet miserable wife alone can be called such.

He has lost position after position in business, until he is found in the very gutters of our streets.

And as he lies there he is pointed at as an exhibition of the Devil's work; he has "gone to the Devil."

Is it not true? Is not this exactly the common popular idea as to the Devil's work? Indeed it is.

But the victim may be a woman. We will not go into the sad details of the picture of what we are accustomed to regard as the Devil's work with regard to the gentler sex. All that is truly beautiful is gone, all that is womanly is obscured, and—in no lightness let it be spoken—nor will we speak as men speak of her, as the "unfortunate," but we will use the plain word of Scripture; and in the "harlot" we find a picture of what is commonly regarded as "the Devil's work."

Now, if this conception is not, when thus expressed, absolutely *opposed* to the truth of Scripture, it is at least so far defective as to be a very serious error. I would like to put before you a picture of two men, and ask you to tell me which, in your judgment, is the best exhibition of the work of the Devil.

The first is by no means a choice character. He has not gone to the length of the supposed case above; but still you will find him in the saloon;

very probably he will be the proprietor of the saloon. His name is not on any church roll. He is loose in life, profane in lip, careless of decencies. He is indeed "hail-fellow-well-met" with every one, but yet truly esteemed by none. He is what is usually called "disreputable" by the refined, educated or religious classes, an "honest fellow" by his associates, who find it difficult to conceive of *honesty* in such a world as this apart from defiant ungodliness.

We will put him on one side, and now let me bring before you a man of the highest respectability and self-complacency. He is a "church member," and prides himself, not a little, on the fact.

Indeed we may safely go still further in these days, and see in him a very pillar of the church; an elder, whose wealth alone, with its consequent standing in the business, and influence in the social world, have given him this office; perhaps we may go still higher; he may even be called "The Rev." or "The Very Rev.," or what-not; it is not the position but the character, we seek to look at. Wherever he is, every breath of flattery that blows his way he appropriates to himself as his undoubted due. He is, if a man of affairs, exceedingly fond of that utterly misquoted and mis-used text, that perhaps more than any other has been bedraggled in the mire of man's covetousness, "be diligent in business."* Nor

---

*Rom. xii:11 should read as in R. V. *"in diligence not slothful,"* this is: throw your heart into all you do; but be careful of motive and direction, *"fervent i' spirit, serving the Lord."*

does he shrink from any little sacrifice that shall secure the greater esteem of his fellow-men; like all else his benefactions are "respectable;" and, if he be very wealthy, they may appear princely.

Now which of these two is the truest example of the Devil's work?

It will probably be admitted that the first may be accepted as an exact representation of what the Devil can do with a man, but it is difficult to see in the second any exhibition of the Devil's work at all. Quite the contrary; he is a respectable religious member of society; perhaps with some of the lesser defects inherent amongst men; but not to be associated with the Devil at all. Let us see.

Once, "two men went up into the temple to pray, the one a pharisee and the other a publican." In daily life in the past, as well as in social position, they answered very fairly to the two pictures given above. And now listen to the verdict that the Lord Jesus Christ pronounces as He hears their differing ways of approach. You remember it.— Was it quite in accord with the view expressed above? Was it? Does it confirm or reverse that view as to which is the truest expression of the Devil's work; the Publican or a Pharisee?

It will probably be said: "He did not approve the life or character of the publican, but his confession. And this is quite true; but the rejection of the respectable religious man, *without one single feature that men regard as the Devil's work,* is the point in view here.

But further, it is a most striking fact that when our Lord Jesus was on earth, He never, in one single instance, witnessed to the publican and harlot that their deeds were evil? We may wonder why He did not, but it is quite sure He did not. And why? Surely because it was unnecessary. That kind of people knew it well then, and know it well, now, of themselves, without any one else telling them. But to whom does He witness that their deeds are evil, and they hate Him on account of that witness (John vii:7)? In the 23rd chapter of Matthew we read the sternest words that ever fell from those blessed lips. He calls those to whom He speaks—the men of the most rigid religious correctness, men of the highest social respectability, of the greatest formal piety and religious pretension; not merely "church-members" as we should now call them, but the officers, deacons, elders, clergymen, priests, bishops, archbishops, cardinals, popes of that day, *"fools and blind," "blind guides," "hypocrites,"* until, in the climax of His holy indignation, He says, *"Ye serpents, ye generation of vipers, how can ye escape the damnation of hell?"** *

*It is surely hardly necessary to guard this by saying that humble and penitent believers; and devoted and lowly ministers of God's Word, are by no means even hinted at as being included in this category, irrespective of what ecclesiastical connection or position they may be in. Nor on the other hand is it questioned for a moment that the

SATAN.

This is strong language that testifies to "evil deeds," does it not? Oh, surely, it must have been a very serious disease that necessitated such heroic treatment.—Aye indeed, for this was in the far off day of Cain; was then in the day of the Lord Jesus; is today, and will be to the end, the *"way that seemeth right to a man, but the end thereof are the ways of death"* (Prov. xiv:12).

It is, then, the testimony of God's Word, whether we are prepared to accept it or not, that it is the proud, religious, self-complacent character that is a truer expression of the Devil's work amongst men than the openly profane and morally debased.

This is so utterly contrary, not merely to what is recognized in business circles, but to what is taught from the bulk of Christian pulpits, that it is difficult to sufficiently press the importance of giving it careful and candid consideration.

I trust enough at least has been said to loosen our minds somewhat from prejudice, or popular teaching, or mere tradition; and permit us, with candor, to see further what the teachings of Scripture are on this point.

It may be necessary to remind ourselves as to what we have already learned as to the crime of the Devil; for his subsequent work amongst men will, in all probability, bear the same character.

Devil may, and does use *the flesh* in men, in all its various character of evil, for his purposes.

ITS ROOT CHARACTER.

That sin we are plainly told in 1 Tim. iii:6 was *"being puffed up with pride;"* and this corresponds so exactly with the words that we have considered in Ezek. xxviii:17, "thine heart was lifted up;" and again in Is. xiv, "thou hast said in thine heart I will be like the Most High," that we need surely have no hesitation not only in recognizing this *pride* as the Devil's primal iniquity, but the Root or Pattern Sin of the universe, and to characterize his work amongst men.

Nor does it militate against this that men either think lightly of it, or positively admire it as a virtue, or that it is not an offence on the statute books of any country upon earth. Indeed, if it were—if pride were a penal offence in civilized society, who would be left to administer justice? The dock would be filled, the Bench would be empty; and none but a few of the meek, and these self-confessed sinners, who are not even known, or thought of, would be left to "inherit the earth." Well, there is a word that looks very much as if that would, one day, be the case exactly (Matt. v:5).

But it is not human courts with which we have to do. *"Everyone of us shall give account of himself to God;"* and in that court, the chief or Root sin is not lying, thieving, impurity, drunkenness, far less the comparatively petty things; which, being in measure free from themselves, men and women, in their legality and folly, exalt to the place of prominence; but the poor vain creature exalting himself to the place of independence of the Creator. This is the Root of all; the others follow as consequences; and God ever exposes the Root, the fruit will then take care of itself.

From the nature of his own crime, from what is all pervasive in the world; we are prepared to look for the work of the devil as being of this *root* character; leading men into independence and distrust of God, to believe any lie however subtle or however foolish, rather than to put perfect confidence in the Word of the God who *cannot* lie.

CHAPTER XI.

THE DEVIL'S FIRST WORKS WITH MEN.

Contents.

With our mind thus open to receive whatever the
Scriptures may give us, let us look very briefly at
the first work of the Devil with mankind, for like
all *firsts* in God's Word, it will afford an excellent
pattern of all that follows. Nor, frequently as we
have gone over the thrilling story of that "battle of
Eden," as we may call it, shall we find that we have
exhausted either its interest or value.

Let us then open our Bibles together at Gen. iii,
and note a few points from the meagre, yet pregnant
details there recorded for us.

First we have the third *speaker*: the serpent
talks! It is one of the points that awakens the profane ridicule of the impious and bold infidelity of
our day. Yet assume for the sake of argument that
a spirit *had* taken possession of this serpent, could
he more surely evidence his presence than by

speech? For speech as we have before noted is the faculty of the *spirit*, by which the mind is communicated. There is no speech connected with the body, even when there is the principle of life, as in a tree; nor with the *soul*, as in beasts, birds, and fishes. This must therefore be confined to the spirit, for there alone is the capacity for either apprehending, or requiring apprehension of the highest quality of the creature; reason. The speech then of the serpent is in perfect harmony with all that we now know as to the *spirit*, and proves exactly what all Scripture, to the very end, asserts, that we have here, the one who is now called the Devil, tempting Eve by his subtlety; yea, the *old Serpent*.

That he should make his attack on the woman, when apart from her husband, is also fully in line with all that we now know of his ways of falsehood. Still is the mistake, that Milton puts into Eve's mouth, manifest

> "Nor much expect
> A foe so proud will first the weaker seek."

for this is exactly what he does. And still will error ever seek in the weaker, the line of least resistance; while Truth ever longs for the strongest light in which it thrives, nor fears the strongest foe. Paul, in resisting the early inroads of legality, seeks no weaker foe than Peter the "pillar," whom he withstands to his face (Gal. ii); whilst it is the easily-led "woman" that the opposing Jews stir up

(Acts xiii:50). And Satan rejoices to find Eve at a distance from her husband. Again, in the words of Milton,

> "Then let me not let pass
> Occasion which now smiles; behold alone
> The woman, opportune to all attempts."

Nor is it without significance, nor does it fail to add its measure of testimony to the truth of these first chapters of Genesis, that in all the recently developed phases of old heresies, women have largely been the media of their promulgation. In fancied independence, out of her place, as Eve, she is open to the wily assaults of the enemy, and he still uses her in the same way as he did then, as witness Madame Blavatsky, Mrs. Besant, Mrs. Eddy and her women supporters, or rivals, and the many spirit "mediums," nearly all of whom are women.

We will not go over the familiar scene in detail here; but there is one feature in it, not frequently noticed, that bears so directly on our theme that we must not pass it. It consists in the *silences* and *omissions* in the Serpent's address. It is not the Devil who tells Eve that the forbidden Tree is *"good for food."* She comes to that conclusion herself, whilst he, in his normal condition of *spirit,* has no fleshly body to feed. It is not the Devil who points out that it is "pleasant to the eyes"; she is perfectly competent to discover that herself; indeed far more so than her *soul-less* tempter: for the eye is the outlet of the soul. But how does she learn that it is a tree to be desired *"to make wise,"* except, and alone, in the light of his words: *"for God doth know that in the day that ye shall eat thereof, then your eyes shall be opened, and ye shall be as God (not gods) knowing good and evil."* This is distinctly the temptation to her *spirit;* and he, a *spirit,* is thus leading her in the very path of pride that he himself, as we have seen, had gone, to be "as God." He was instilling the same mind in her that was in himself, whilst loosening her mind from its confidence in the love of God, in His care for her.

So it is common for people to-day to pass on to to the Devil all that is distinctly of their own responsibility; whilst quite complacently appropriating to themselves what is *his* work. They would fain quiet conscience by attributing to him all their fleshly depravity, sensual indulgence, or worldly lust. The publican and harlot; the drunkard and the libertine, knowing well the evil of their way, plead that that is due to the "temptations of the Devil"! Nay, it needs no Devil for this, in their case any more than in Eve's; for these come from those parts of their being, not shared at all, normally, by the evil spirit. Whilst what is really *his* work, the sense of self-complacency, whether it springs from an external morality or an official superiority, or religious associations, is not recognized as such at all, for is not this way ever "right to a man"? Yet, alas! "the end of that way is *death,"* for it is most effectual in keeping from God. Nor was there ever a time when this awful mistake was more widespread. My dear reader, let us see that it be not the case with us.

The Serpent's address to Eve is marvellous in its subtle skill: *"Yea truly,"* he says, "is it possible that God has said to one so fair and noble" (for this is implied in the opening words), *"ye shall not eat of every tree of the garden."* If even in Eden, with everything on every hand to tell of love and solicitous care, he could point to one single prohibition—place it in such prominence, "in the midst," as to eclipse everything else, and thus drive a wedge between the heart's confidence and God, surely we may see the method he still takes with men when providences so often tell another story.

But enough, the bait to be "as God" does its work, and whilst Adam is not deceived as Eve, discerns full well the evil consequences of eating; yet are his affections Godward weak; and he,

> "Scrupled not to eat,
> Against his better knowledge; not deceived
> But fondly overcome with female charm."

His heart, as hers, has lost its home in God; it is the Devil's work: his pattern work through all time. His work with you and me this very hour, my dear reader.

Now for one glance at the first work *after* this Fall, and indeed the comment of the Apostle on the murder of Abel connects it directly with our subject:

"Not as Cain, who was of that wicked one, and slew his brother. And wherefore slew he him? Because his own works were evil, and his brother's righteous."

What were these evil works of Cain? The ordinary popular answer is that Cain's life was bad. But surely it was not because he was a drunkard, or profane, or a libertine that he slew Abel; yea, even that *murder* is not, in itself, his evil work, but the result of it. He murdered *because* his works were evil. The narrative in Genesis answers the question clearly—awfully clearly—his evil works were his *good works!* It was because of the rejection of his offering that he was wroth and his countenance fell, and he slew his brother.

And Abel's "righteous works," what were they? God Himself tells us, for he witnessed—not of his life or conduct—but "of his gifts that he was righteous" (Heb. xi:3).

Cain was not one whit less religious than Abel; not one word is said as to any inferiority in his morality. If we were speaking in the phraseology of the Lord's time we should say that they both "went up to the temple to pray"; if of this day, they both went equally to a place of worship, or attended church: were equally religious men. The only difference was in that by which they approached God. Cain's offering said "I have done

my best; what more can any man do? It is true it
is the fruit of a cursed earth; but can I help that?
A *curse* is all that God has given, and I only bring
the result of the sweat of my brow, my work, here
Thou has that is Thine, what can man do more?"

Abel's offering said "I have heard a sweeter story
far than that from my father's lips and at my
mother's knee: how God has far more than a curse
to give; for if it was He who provided the skins
that covered them, so I work not; but, ungodly, I
confess my helplessness, and the Lamb, His gift,
dies in my stead, and so again God's love provides
what covers me: blessed be His Name."

And so Jehovah speaks to wrathful Cain: *"If
thou doest well,"* that is, dost confess that simple
truth as to thyself, and bring a propitiatory offering, *"shalt thou not be accepted? And if thou dost
not well,"* that is if thou bringest thine own works,
"sin* lieth at the door." It is not removed. Sin

---

*The word for Sin is used also for "Sin-offering," and
the passage is so interpreted by many; but it would be
quite out of place so to render it here; and that for at
least three reasons: *first* we hear nothing at all of a Sin-
offering before the giving of the law, the burnt offering
seems then to have covered the idea of propitiation for
sin (Job i:5) and *secondly* because, if the "doing not well"
referred, as it clearly did, to the offerings, then it would be
really unintelligible to say "if thy *offering* does not witness to thy confession of thyself as a sinner; *then, in
that case,* it follows as a consequence that a sin offering
is at the door"! This would be meaningless: and *thirdly*
because of the entire suitability of the rendering "Sin,"

blocks the entrance: thou canst not reach me, I cannot get to thee in blessing: for "without the shedding of blood there is no remission of sins."

Here then is why Cain was of that wicked one, the Devil; not because he was not religious, or refrained from attending a place of worship; but simply because his bloodless offering showed the same evidence of the Devil's work in proud self-complacency, as did practically the same thing in the pharisee in the temple, and does in the Christless clergy and church members of our day.

The Devil has sent, is sending, myriads in the way of Cain, to the temple, to the church; but never from the beginning of the world, to the present day, nor as long as he works amongst men, will he work in any heart the cry, *God be merciful to me a sinner,* for that is the way of Abel, and the first righteous word a sinful child of Adam can ever speak; and at once God meets him with the Ransom He has found (Job xxxiii:24).

---

and its harmony with clear Scripture, such as *"your iniquities have separated between you and your God"* (Is. lix:2) *they* were at the door still, *preventing God reaching him in blessing, or he reaching God with acceptance.*

CHAPTER XII.

Contents.

We have looked back at the first works of the Devil with man, let us use the prophetic scriptures we hold in our hands, and, with the one and sole idea of seeing their character, look forward to his last works at the end of this dispensation; and if we find them to be of exactly the same nature, we may confidently affirm that we have the main features of those works through all of the ages of time.

In nothing is the teaching of seducing spirits, and doctrine of demons, made more manifest than in the wide-spread and popular belief that the present age is to end in universal blessing, prosperity, and advancement of every character: material, moral and spiritual.

This is indeed seductive, for it chimes in well with the inherent pride of the flesh; and on all sides to-day we hear the notes of boasting, and self-congratulation on the "progress" of the times.

97

SATAN.

That the activity of the mind of man is effecting, as it has ever done, marvellous achievements in the line of invention, it would be folly to deny. He has almost annihilated distance, and makes his voice to be heard a thousand miles away, and more, with perfect ease. The air, too, and water, are owning his powers in a way hitherto unknown. In the former, he is beginning to rival the birds by his aeroplanes, as in the latter he compares with the denizens of the deep by his submarines: indeed, he is still seeking out "many inventions": and people look at all this, swell up with pride, and call it "progress"!

Is it? How shall we measure progress? One would say from any common sense standpoint, it must be in the attainment, or at least in the evident nearer approach to the goal sought; and that goal may be called *perfect satisfaction,* leaving nothing to be desired.

The evidence of *progress* would then be *increasing contentment;* the restless working of man's longing becoming

> "Merely as the working of a sea
> Before a calm, that rocks itself to rest."

Is this the case? Let any one of candor judge. Are people more satisfied, more content, more happy than they were? Let the ever sharper conflicts between Labor and Capital answer. Let the ever increasing crowds of unemployed in the big cities reply. Let the uses to which the very inventions are put, as soon as they come into existence, add their witness—war, putting its hand on aeroplane and submarine, and on every invention that can possibly serve its turn, saying "it is mine." Nay, the very fact of invention itself has a voice that does not negative all these other witnesses, for it is a true saying, "necessity is the mother of invention." There was no invention in Eden, for there was *no need*. The fall introduces the inventive faculty, and human ingenuity begins to work to overcome the need, of which now for the first time, man becomes aware; but we hear no singing in connection with this first *invention* of the apron of fig leaves. That faculty of invention has marked man's path throughout the centuries. Not always at one level, or ever moving in one direction,—it has risen and fallen as the tides; now surging upward with skillful "artifices in brass and iron," and to the music of "harp and organ," until it aims at heaven itself, and again and again the Lord interposes and abases by flood or scattering— now ebbing, till apparently extinct in the low-sunken tribes of earth. Its activity is the accompaniment usually of the light God gives, and which man turns to his own boasting, with no recognition of the Giver; calling it "Civilization." The Lord's people are not, for the most part, found in the line of inventors. The seed of Cain, and not of Seth produces them. The former make the earth their home; and, as "the dwellers upon earth" naturally seek to beautify it and make it comfortable. The latter, with deepest soul-thirst quenched by rills of living water springing not here; with heart-longings satisfied by an infinite, tender, divine Love, pass through the earth, strangers and pilgrims, to the Rest of God. In view of this, does the very phenomenon of intense activity in the sphere of invention speak of satisfaction and rest, or the reverse? Is it, therefore, a sign of true progress?

It will, of course, be said that our picture of the "goal" is insipid and vacuous. What! No ambition! No motive for effort or energy! Nothing to be attained! Away with such a dull and prosaic elysium.

Do not be distressed; this shall not be, for *"Discovery* shall abide, after *Invention* has vanished away—constant, never-ceasing discovery; the unfolding hour by hour, and age by age, of a Beauty that is infinite and inexhaustible,—the tasting of a new and entrancing perfection in a Love in which every moment shows some fresh attraction, some new sweet compulsion to praise."

But take another standpoint, and from it judge the pretensions of modern Progress. Is the framework of society more closely held together by reverence for authority in the state, by reverence of youth for age in the social world, by reverence of children for parents in the family? There is but one answer possible to truth or candor. It is quite the reverse. The spirit of democracy, whatever its advantages, is not the foster-mother of reverence.

HIS LAST WORKS.

Finally, from the only sure, solid, certain standpoint of Scripture, is there true progress? What does the word of God clearly teach us to expect in the last days—are they to be the best? Are we to glide sweetly by the constant triumph of truth into a millennium of a spiritual reign? There is not one letter of Scripture to give basis for such a thought. On the contrary, "The last days" are to be "perilous" (2 Tim. iii:1) and if that were the only word bearing on the subject, it is so clear, so unequivocal, so pertinent, as to be conclusive. But it only harmonizes with all others. *"The Spirit speaketh expressly that in the latter times*—not 'many shall come to.,' but *some shall depart from the faith"* (1 Tim. iv:1). And if the days of Lot, and of Noah, were such as to introduce blessing and not judgment, then the last days of this dispensation shall be the same; but not otherwise, for they are to be as those days.

This brings us directly to our point, the last works of the Devil amongst men at the end of this dispensation. The Apostle, in writing to the young believers at Thessalonica, says: *"For that day shall not come except there come the apostasy first, and that man of sin be revealed, the son of perdition, who opposeth and exalteth himself above all that is called God, or that is worshipped; so that he sitteth in the temple of God, showing himself that he is God."*

It will not be necessary to go into any detailed

examination of this solemn Scripture—it will be enough to note the clear links with the Devil's first work in Eden. There the bait was *"ye shall be as God"*; here the claim is to being God indeed; and can any one doubt the true author of that claim? It is the Devil's work in full-blown perfection.

And that claim is not made in heathendom, but in the sphere where the Lord Jesus Christ has been professedly owned in the professing church, or Christendom. Here is such an awful departure from truth that it is called "the apostasy": not only is truth turned away from, but the spirit of pride and self-exaltation current on all sides to-day, comes to its head in man claiming to be God.*

Thus Satan at the first, and Satan at the last, drags his victim, man, in his own path of pride; of complete self-sufficiency and independency—and that, on one form or another, is the surest, clearest, characteristic of his work all through the ages.

And ever more actively does he work amongst us on these lines as his day draws to its close; for that which is night to us, is day to him; and the

---

*Mr. Philip Mauro in his last book, "The Number of Man," which has been published since the above was written, shows, with great clearness and power, the rapidity with which all the movements that may be termed characteristic of the present day, such as Socialism, Trades-Unionism, Trusts, New Theology, Modernism, are all tending up to one focus-point: *the deification of man.* And he asks, with much pertinency, must there not be one master-mind shaping all? If so, whose is it?

day for us shall be for him the night when he works no more. For us, believers, the night is far spent, the day draws nigh—for him the reverse. Aware of this, what his hand finds to do, he is indeed doing "with his might," and the ever louder expressions of that first sin of his: pride, only now from human lips, proves, little as the poor boasters think it, their complete subjection to the Devil and his will; which they, although the learned, the wise, the great, the noble, of earth, as well as the masses that either follow, or contend with them for their own interests, are all doing, and will do, till He come.

CHAPTER XIII.

TWO CONTRASTED WORKS.

Contents.

Two opposite works equally of the Devil.—Amalgamation and division.—The Tower of Babel.—Present Babylon. —The Devil's gathering and scattering to-day.

Incidentally there are two opposite yet equally clearly marked phases of the Devil's work, which are closely connected with that same root-sin: pride. In every way his work is the very opposite of that of the Lord Jesus. In the way he leads men he practically says, "let this mind be in you which was also in me; who, being but a creature, grasped at being as God"; whilst the mind that was in Christ Jesus, to whom it was no robbery to be equal with God, led, and still leads, in quite the contrary path of esteeming "others better than" ourselves (Phil. ii). God grant us grace to follow it!

Thus the two "works" are in direct opposition. The Lord Jesus died that He might "gather together in one the children of God that are scattered abroad" (John xi:52). Are we to be surprised, then, if, whilst the Devil is to-day, on the one hand, binding together in various ways all that is *op-posed* to God, uniting men by selfish interests into confederacies, trusts, unions, societies, yet, on the other, he is ever aiming at destroying practical unity wherever it *does* exist amongst the children of God; and thus, as far as lies in his power, un-doing the work of the Son of God. Let us briefly consider both these.

In a far-off past, men, journeying down from the highlands of the East, found a level plain, "and *they dwelt there*." It was the plain of Shinar, the pecu-liar abode of wickedness (Zech. v), and finding that it promised to supply all that their lower na-tures craved, they would build a "city and a tower." The materials were at hand. They had lost the stone of the mountains they had left, it is true; but they could replace this with bricks of their own manufacture, and of the same material as them-selves; and use a vile "slime for mortar." "Go to," they cry, "let us build up a city and a tower whose top may reach to heaven, and let us make us a name, lest we be scattered." There is to be really no limit to the height of his building, it shall take man up "to heaven," or make him as God.

But Another observes the work, and the "Go to" of men is met by the "Go to" of God; and lo, in an hour, has all their building come to naught, and they are scattered.

Surely these things are an allegory; for it is the professing Church's path in figure. In her course divinely told us in Rev. ii, iii, she, too, leaves the mountainous East—the place of divine and moral elevation—and comes down to the ease of this world and dwells at last "where Satan's throne is." There she seeks to unify the race, not with "living stones," as at first, but mere clay, i. e., man in a state of nature. She makes these into "bricks" by her own awful method of "hardening." No new birth is needed, no quickening of the Spirit of God. But she binds her materials together with the vile slime of self-interest or superstitious fear. That first Babel is only later Babylon, and Babylon is only the false harlot church that heads up in Rome, and may be discerned in the woman who teaches in Thyatira (Rev. ii:20).

But God has scattered, and the 1,500 or more sects of Protestantism are the many "tongues"—none able to understand the other—witness of His intervention in judgment. But these shall all be brought together again. When an Image shall be set up by a "King of Babylon" that shall command the prostration of all "peoples, nations, and languages" (Dan. iii and Rev. xiii). What God scatters, the Devil unites. What God would gather in one, he would scatter. *Denominations* he is now seeking to coalesce, and no very keen prophetic vision is needed to see the platform that shall be broad enough to permit not only the various Protestant sects, not only Protestant and Romanist, but even Jew and Christian to stand together upon it—at one at last in the rejection of all the divine claims of Jesus Christ come in the flesh. It is even hardly prophecy for every week sees a nearer approach to such a condition of things.

But strangely enough, every week, too, sees the result of the Devil's activity on the other side; an ever increasing disruption amongst the true children of God. We see not only true and genuine Christians of the same neighborhood, but at times those of the same family, separating, on some comparatively petty plea, on Sunday morning, to worship the same God at different places. Thus proclaiming to a scoffing world that the truths they hold in common as to the Person and Work of their one common Saviour, are not as important to unite them, as the questions wherein they differ—as, for example, the subjects for, or the amount of water to be used, or the form of its application, in baptism, or some other equally momentous an issue (their name is legion)—are to separate. Is it not a shame that may well abase us to the dust? Can one doubt but that this is the Devil's work?

We might do well to consider what the Apostle Paul said when a similar danger threatened in Corinth, if I may paraphrase: "My beloved brethren, let me get my arm close round you; whatever you do I am with you in it. When you restore that erring brother, I have done so already, so that we will not let Satan get an advantage over us by separating us one from another, for we are not ignorant of his devices" (2 Cor. ii). But I fear *we* are densely "ignorant of his devices," if we think that his work is confined to the profane and the harlot, and are blind to the fact that one form of it is to *scatter* those whom the Lord died to *gather* together in one; and oh, how, by our wicked folly, he has succeeded—has he not?

It must not for a moment be allowed that there is not a divinely formed unity in the church of God, that is forever irrefragable by the malice or subtlety of either the Devil or man; and it needs but a touch of some keen trial, or deep sorrow, for all these humanly constructed barriers to be shattered as the vain things they are—at least temporarily. Death comes close to one of the members of the Body of Christ, and no power can keep the others from expressing their sympathy and affection in the most tender way, even with those to whom they would, in submission to some utterly unscriptural "principle," forbid a place at the Lord's Table. How often has it been said, "it takes a funeral to bring the Lord's people together in these days; the showing forth *His* death will not do it!" Yet, underneath all, the one common Life in Christ, with its common confidences, interests, hopes and dangers must lead to more or less clearly expressed external unity. Alas, alas, that it is "less" rather than "more."

It is now nearly a century since many Christians were led to disavow as sin all the manifested disruptions in the professing Church; going so far as to refuse any name that would distinguish them from other Christians. They would be known as "brethren,"* since this was a scriptural appelation, spoke of one common parentage, predicated one life shared in common by all. But it is just amongst these that the schisms they so earnestly repudiated have been reduplicated: division after division has been effected; party after party has been formed; and none can estimate the anguish that has wrung the hearts of the rank and file of these beloved people of God at each one. Many have gone and are going down to the end of their life with the thick shadow of this sorrow over them. Whilst we can but recognize in this human sin and failure; yet it is impossible not to discern the only one whose keen subtlety could alone account for so striking—yes almost incredible a phenomenon: it is the Devil's work.

It will need nothing less than the Lord Jesus Himself to come again, and give that shout that shall gather every one of His heavenly redeemed "from the earth, from the tomb," to Himself, to 'bring to nothing" *this* work of the Devil. But whilst this is true, we must be careful not to play into his hands by governing our own path, or limiting our affections, or indeed letting them be chilled

---

*The term "Plymouth brethren" was given by outsiders who did not understand the principle involved, but it was never accepted by those who did.

by any humanly constructed system, under whatever name, inclusive of less than the whole mystic Body of Christ, for this is nothing else or less than *sin.*

God, in His infinite compassion and grace, has made full provision for the simplest of His people to walk with Himself, even through the intensified confusion of the present day, and down to the very end, by clearly providing both the centre and circumference of their communion. The *centre,* the name of the Lord Jesus Christ (Matt. xviii:20) ; the *circumference,* every recognized, or evidenced member of His mystic body (Ephes. iv:4).

But we must not follow this interesting subject further here; but return to our main theme.

CHAPTER XIV.

SOME MODERN INSTANCES.

Contents.

In considering the work of the Devil it is impossible to overestimate the subtlety with which his attacks are made; always when least expected, where least expected, and how least expected, and we may confidently affirm that in such a day of his activity in which our lot is cast, not one whose eyes are not in some measure anointed with the eye-salve the Lord Jesus gives will be able to discern him in the apparently lovely and winning forms he assumes.

Look at a striking illustration of this in Scripture. The Lord had told His disciples for the first time of the Cross to which He was going (Matt. xvi:21). Peter, who has just been pronounced blessed, begs Him not to think of such a thing. "This shall be far from" Him. Which of us would not have said that this was the language of genuine affection and tender solicitude? *He* said "Get thee behind me, *Satan!*" We should have said "how kind! how amiable! how good!" He said "how Satanic!"

Are we not compelled to gather from this, and does it not confirm what we have seen, that whoever, or whatever, tends to put aside the atoning work of the Cross is utterly Satanic? It is a hard saying to many; but judged in the light of this incident, where would a large number of our modern, popular clergymen appear? Amiable in disposition, eloquent in speech, gracious in deportment, they never disturb the false peace of their congregations with a hint that they are not all children of God; they never offend the ear with reference to a judgment to come nor breathe a word of the "Severity of God," the Lake of Fire, and coming wrath. They are "practical;" and, avoiding doctrine, they dwell much on practical righteousness, but with no remedy however for past failures in it. They love to speak of civic-righteousness and to guide the votes of their flocks in this world's politics. They do not teach that Jesus died as a substitutionary sacrifice for lost sinners; and if ever they do speak and write on such a text as *"My God, my God, why hast thou forsaken me,"* it is in order to prove that the Speaker was mistaken; and under the natural depression of the hour, He spoke what was not true.*

Well, as God is true; as the Scriptures are His Word; as the Lord Jesus Christ is His Son, this is, in spite of all its offsetting attraction, essentially Satanic; and woe to those who can sit complacently under such teaching.

But let us again "go to Church." Contemplate before we enter, the architectural beauty of that

---

*An actual and recent (but by no means isolated) fact; by a Congregational clergyman of Montclair, N. J.

grand edifice: let the "dim religious light" as we open the door, throw its gentle chastening over our spirit; mark the long-drawn aisles, the fretted canopies; harken to the solemn swell of the organ; the scent of incense lends its aid; listen to the sweet sound of human voices from the highly-paid choir—all serving to bear our souls aloft on the wings of deep religious feeling, till emotion fills our eyes with tears. Ah, it is hard to say that tested by its bearing on Christ and His cross, it is essentially Satanic, for it fills the so-called worshippers with delusive self-satisfaction, and soothes them with a sleep that must have an awful awakening. Far from humbling man, it puffs him up; far from exalting Christ, it practically excludes Him. It is, in spite of its religion, utterly Satanic.*

Take the field of modern popular literature. Does one need to descend to the filth of the impure

---

*Let this not be misunderstood as asserting that Christ. and the virtues of His Cross, may not be preached in some measure, in such places. This surely may be, and at times is the case, and very thankful may we be for it. But this is rather in *spite* of, than *because* of this unscriptural lingering in the shadows of a past Judaism: this feeble copying of a once divinely ordained, but now superseded ritual. It is by such things as these that men *"say they are Jews and are not"* (Rev. ii:9) : going back to a day of shadows that is now past, since Christ, the Substance of all, has come (Col. ii:16, 17). It is the substitution of the sensuous for the spiritual in worship, to which reference is made in the text as Satanic, as it surely is. Nor is there any intention of condemning simple musical aids to congregational singing. Such condemnation would be worse than its object.

French novel to find the Devil's work? Not at all. Not even the bold naked infidel writings of Germany have any monopoly of his authorship. There is no need to go beyond our own country, for in the most respectable newspapers, in the most widely circulated and best edited magazines, there is hardly an issue in our day that does not contain some thrust, open or covert, at the foundation truths of our holy faith; it is, in spite of its cleverness the Devil's work.

Even in the religious and semi-religious novel of the day, that is so intensely popular, there are the same characteristic marks, skilfully interwoven with much that is commendable. As, for instance, people read that winsome story "The Bonnie Briar Bush," and similar books, the emotions are touched at the tenderly pathetic pictures so skilfully drawn and the eye floods with sympathetic tears, but how open does the reader become to receive with approval the sneer at the doctrine of the total depravity of man; or the skilfully painted parody on the severity of God, and eternal punishment. Do such books, attractive as they are, ever make the Cross of Christ dearer? Do they make Him better known? How can they, when man's guilt is minimized and his danger is hidden or denied? What need of Christ and His Cross in that case? This is, in spite of the acknowledged beauty in which it is enwrapped, the Devil's work.

Let us come still nearer, and apply our test to some of the so-claimed evangelical literature of our day. Here we may be thrown quite off our guard by the most earnest and even enthusiastic expressions of devout piety; of devotion to the Bible as the Word of God; of loud rejection of many of the current errors of the day; can all this be linked with Satanic work? Aye, when under all, may be discerned a subtly veiled attack on the Person or Work of the Lord Jesus Christ. Of this character is the teaching of Zion's Watchtower, Christ adelphianism and its kindred errors, not omitting that marvelously successful delusion, Christian Science. It is, in spite of its bold claims, all horribly Diabolic.

Once more, wherever men make a pedantic parade of their learning; and are forever correcting the accepted versions of the Scriptures with references to the original languages, in which they know well their simple hearers are quite unable to prove or disprove their assertions; and this, not merely to enforce or elucidate, but to bring in 'divers and strange doctrines," it is at least safe to be much on our guard, for in spite of the assumed learning, it bears the hall-mark of the Devil's work, in his primal sin, pride; or the human form of it, overweening conceit and vanity.

One can hardly omit any reference to the character or trend of the *philanthropic works* of the day. No longer does kindly and wealthy piety send its help to the *bodies* of the poor, in those rows of comfortable cottages one sees in England, there called almshouses; far less often are large sums given to the spread of the gospel; but, to-day, almost fabulous amounts are diverted solely to the increase of *human intelligence;* but with either avowed rejection of all relationship with God, or in the promulgation of awful soul-destroying error. One would not surely ignore or minimize the kindly sentiment that may lead to the scattering of libraries over the country; but it is no unkindness to say that increased knowledge of God is neither sought nor attained by such gifts. Whilst the millions that, it is claimed, have been won by pitiless destruction of others, are now going to an institution that is as a very fountain-head of poisonous waters, in its bold blasphemy of everything characteristically Christian. It is, in spite of its assumed philanthropy the Devil's work, for does it not remind us of that early "philanthropist" who, in Eden, also desired the increase of human knowledge?

But why should we say in *spite of* attractiveness, religiousness, cleverness, beauty, boldness, philanthropy, or learning? Would not all that we have seen of Satan lead us to expect just such qualities? Are they not in harmony with all that we have learned as to our most subtle foe? Surely they are. Then should we be justified in saying, not "in spite of," but rather *because of* these features that can attract, or soothe, or win the natural man, they are the most fitting instruments for the Devil's work.

Beloved brethren who read these lines, has the Spirit of God written in vain that the last days are perilous or difficult? It is just these beautiful and attractive features that make them so.

CHAPTER XV.

Contents.

Returning to our main subject, let us go one step further—and a very important step it is— and ask, if the crime of the Devil was pride, as it undoubtedly was, what form of expression was it possible for that pride to take? Could it be by any rivalry with any other creature, even with the highest angelic principalities? Impossible: for if even Michael the Archangel acknowledged his superior dignity, it must have been far from "robbery" for him to esteem himself equal with the angels. In all the universe, as far as we can learn from Scripture, there was no creature above him. It would therefore necessarily follow, since there was no possible way that one can see, by which his pride could be expressed, save by grasping at or robbery (as Phil. ii puts it, when dealing with the blessed Contrast) of a position *above* him, to which he was not entitled; and since there was but One above him—what was left save the being as God?

By the specific and reiterated teaching of Scripture as to his sin, pride; by the clear evidence of those Scriptures of his unrivalled dignity, both in person and office, amongst all creatures; by the equally clear account of the path in which he has led and leads mankind; and finally by the path He who is his direct Contrast walked, as told in Phil. ii, ever going lower and lower till He became obedient unto the most shameful death men could devise—by all these reasons combined, we feel assured, tremendous as are the consequences, that his sin was expressed by *direct rivalry with God.*

And further, as we remember Ezek. xxviii and that divine word that addresses him as the *"Cherub that covereth";* and which we have already considered; as we connect this with the only possible expression of his sin as written above, we are forced to the conclusion that his awful ambition was the possession of that very Throne of God, he was, by his office of "Cherub that covereth" bound to guard. Do we not see the force of that charge in Is. xiv.

"Thou hast said, I will be *as the Most High,* I will exalt *my throne above* the stars of God," that is his throne will be above all the angelic hosts, and even as the Most High!

Is not such an ambition—stupendous sin as it is—at least worthy of the highest creature? Even in

his sin—in his fall—*could* he be petty or small?
Could any other be either consistent with his person, or indeed *possible?*

This then was the "inquity" found in him, that
resulted in the ruin of his kingdom, and its chaotic
state as see in Gen. i:2.

But God is again active in goodness; and, although Satan is irrecoverably fallen, the earth is re-
newed, reformed; and, in six days' work, fitted to
be the dwelling of another race *"a little lower than
the angels"* whose lowly kinship with the dust may
at least serve to "hide pride from man."

The deposed Prince hears the man Adam installed
as absolute monarch over every part of that earth
once all his own. Is this a checkmate to him? Not
at all. He will, in a wisdom "corrupted" indeed as
Ezek. xxviii speaks, yet far beyond mere human
thoughts, make use of that very creature—so honored, so tenderly beloved as he sees him to be, still
to attain that primal aim of his: the *Throne of God!*

This supplies us with what has been conspicuous
by its absence in all teachings on this subject, not
only with a motive—but one worthy of so highly
endowed and gifted a creature, for seeking to draw
mankind away from God, into sin; and to bring that
race into exactly the same condemnation with *himself.* Rarely do we hear anything at all of *motive;*
and when we do, it is usually so petty, so pitifully
mean, as to be only worthy of a *man,* and that a
very small man. When men make their own god,

it is impossible that he should be beyond their own powers of conception; and he is consequently a very contemptible god, so when they make their own Devil he is as petty as themselves; but this is no more the Devil of Revelation than is the heathen's idol the God of Revelation.

It was not then because he desired the comfort of company in his present or coming misery in the Lake of Fire; nor to gloat over the victims of his malice as sharing his punishment—no, indeed; but by means of this dearly loved creature, man, he conceived the design, not merely to escape all misery himself, but still to attain what might have been thought to have been lost forever, the object of his highest primal ambition, the Throne of God.

But it would be nothing less than carnal impertinence to suggest motives without such proofs as the Scriptures afford; and no other are of the slightest value.

So let us, consider a few of the incidents divinely recorded for us in the Scriptures that may suffice to show us what his design is, and the means by which he seeks to effect it.

In Job, chap. i:6, we are told that "the Sons of God came to present themselves before the Lord." These Sons of God are beyond any serious question, *angels,* for this same term is frequently used in connections that will admit of no alternative. Take for instance Job xxxviii:7 where the parallelism between "Sons of God" and "morning stars" is quite exclusive of any but angels, especially as men at that time had not come into being at all. So see Ps. xxix:1, lxxxix:7; Dan iii:25, &c.*

Men are never called sons of God in the Old Testament, for although every saved soul from the very beginning was undoubtedly born again and was thus a child of God, yet there was no revelation of that happy relationship, which awaited, as so much else, the coming of the Lord Himself. Nay, further, not until the Spirit of God had come, as the Spirit of adoption, did any man ever cry *"Abba Father,"* or were any ever called sons of God.

But this is said to be denied by such texts as Is. xviii:6, *"bring my sons from far, and my daughters from the ends of the earth."* But anyone can see a distinction between the men of a particular nation being called the sons of Jehovah (not God), and the women of that same nation, the daughters of Jehovah: terms of tenderness and endearment on His part, but without any responsive recognition of relationship on theirs—and the term "Sons of God" applied without distinction of sex to all who are a

---

*Gen. vi:2 is no exception: there may be physiological difficulties; but we know so little of the possibilities of angelic existence that we may well leave this. That angels should eat and drink; feed on meat and bread; might certainly involve equal difficulties, but it is clearly stated in Gen. xviii and xix. Thus they appear to have either a power of materializing, and of assuming the functions of a human body; or, indeed, they may have a kind of spiritual body adapted to them as spirits, as some claim.

new creation in Christ Jesus, and each one of those with the spirit of adoption responding "Abba Father." There are no "daughters of God" where the term is used in this way; and to apply it thus in Old Testament is a dispensational anachronism. Thus wherever it is found it must be referred to angels—who being *spirits* are in this filial relation to Him who is "the father of spirits."

But Satan being a "son of God," comes with them, and the Lord addresses, without naming him: "Whence comest thou?" Now the Lord's questions are never for His own enlightenment. He knew well whence he came. Why then ask, except to repudiate his service? If God had sent him on a service, He would never have asked that question.

Satan replies "From going to and fro in the earth and from walking up and down in it."

Throwing the light of what we have already learned on this, we might paraphrase it thus: "Where should I have come from? Hast Thou not, amid all these worlds, put the Earth under *my* care and government; and, consistently with that charge, I have been most diligently searching my dominion through and through, to maintain strict righteousness in it; the righteousness of that Throne I am appointed to cover."

That is, in his answer, he still claims to be the "Cherub that covereth"; to have the supervision of the earth; and be an angel of light with only care for the *maintenance of righteousness.* He has not accepted his deposition. Then the Lord meets him on the ground he assumes, as He ever does, and says as it were, "hast thou been seeking to maintain righteousness in the earth? Well then hast thou considered one righteous man, my servant, Job, who feareth God and eschews evil?

Thus Jehovah puts Job before Satan as a kind of representative—the best that can be found—of the beloved race that has superseded him, and one whose heart is wholly true to God.

If we read the 29th chapter of Job we shall probably recognize that Satan had indeed not only "considered" Job, but had done a good deal of preliminary work with him already. Listen to the poor afflicted man, musing on his past, and hugging to his heart the memory of his many charities: *"When the ear heard me then it blessed me, when the eye saw me, it gave witness to me." "I put on righteousness and it clothed me, my judgment was as a robe and a diadem,"* and so on. Does not that look as if Satan had been at work with Job, puffing him up, and whispering some such flattery as "Oh Job thou art indeed a righteous man; there is none like thee in all the earth; and these strong sons and lovely daughters, these flocks and herds; all this wealth that thou hast acquired; this robust health thou dost enjoy; are all but the just due of thy righteousness; and if they should ever be taken from thee, it would be a gross injustice, and show how little thou art really loved: how little God cares for thee."

Is not that still the way in which he seeks to affect God's people, leading them ever to think highly of themselves, and predisposing them, by his sweet flattery, to think hardly of their Father's chastening dealings with them? Indeed it is, and when loss of property, bereavement of those tenderly loved, wearying sickness or painful disease take the place of health, then we are too often open to listen to that crafty whisper: "And *this* is God's love for thee!"

Satan answers that he has considered Job and discerned that his fidelity is only skin-deep; and if God will but touch Job in the wealth or health He has given him, it will reveal his true condition, and, far from God having his heart, Job will curse Him to His face.

Thus he challenges God to enter into the lists with himself for man's heart; utters a taunt so craftily veiled indeed that it might well sound as merely the exercise of his office of "Cherub that covereth," and that as such, he only desired that so unrighteous a condition of things as the divine appreciation of a non-existent loyalty should cease.

Jehovah accepts the challenge and Job loses everything, till the storm past, in the clear light shining after rain, he sees his Lord with his eye— as it would seem we never do, save through trouble and sorrow—and his heart springs back to Him as a babe to a well-known breast, and he abhors *himself* in dust and ashes, as every dear child of God, sooner or later, does.

This means a defeat for Satan; but we see his aim; to bring the best of men, beloved of God, before the Throne as a *curser,* while he himself, posing as jealous for true righteousness, would see how God could deal with such a case in mercy and righteousness.

Again in the 3rd chap. of Zechariah, we find Joshua, the high-priest, and, as such, the representative, first of Israel, then of the whole race of mankind, standing before the Lord, clothed in filthy garments, and Satan—plainly named now, for here is one whose blessing he may righteously oppose, standing at his side to resist him. In other words we find that Satan has at last got a *representative* man before that Throne of the Lord it was his office to protect from unrighteousness, in exactly the condition suited to his purpose. There is even no possible *pretension* to righteousness here; no fair "robe," or glorious "diadem," nothing but "filthy garments" that speak to every eye, and that tell out, as Adam's fig leaves, the vanity, the defilement of all man's doings. Who now is sufficient to answer Satan? Who can save the poor, silent, self-confessed sinner there? Search through heaven, earth and underworld, and there is none but One and He Himself "God over all, blessed forever." "Change of raiment" and "fair mitre" soon show what He can do. It is a beautiful picture of the divine answer to Satan's purpose, although even yet the full truth is veiled in the term "the angel of the Lord"; who, in the words, "The Lord rebuke thee" confesses that none but God can solve this problem whilst the words *"is not this a brand plucked from the burning."* Must have sounded as merry as a marriage chime to the poor sinner, but as an awful knell in his ears for whom that fire is specifically prepared.

CHAPTER XVI.

(HIS MOTIVE CONTINUED.)

Contents.

Further in considering Satan's motive for constant opposition and accusation of men, let us look at Prov. xvi:12 giving us the very foundation or base of any throne *"The throne is established by righteousness."*

No doubt Solomon had an earthly throne in view; but that this truth equally governs the Throne of God Ps. lxxxix:14 clearly proves. *"Justice and Judgment are the foundation of thy throne."* That is God's Throne is unshakable, cannot be overthrown because it is based, established, on absolute righteousness—nothing contrary to the absolute perfection of divine holiness is permitted, where that Throne is set up.

Suppose then for a moment the possibility of this foundation being changed in its character, even to the smallest degree: suppose the slightest element of injustice, whether in punishing the innocent, or in sparing the guilty, to be introduced; there can be no question but that the foundation would be destroyed—and the Throne—even God's Throne could be shaken, for it has lost its base.

Now turn to Prov. xx:28, *"The Throne is upholden by mercy."* Here the change of the word from "established" in Ch. xvi to "upholden" is not without its significance. The former speaks of the foundation, the latter of "support." A building badly founded will surely fall; but a building simply imposed, even on a rock, if it has no support will also fall. The word for "upholden" has in it the idea of "comfort." "Comfort thine heart," says the Levite's father-in-law to him, using this same word in Judges xix; and the use of it here in Proverbs would suggest that if the King cannot exercise mercy his throne is practically of no use— his will is barred, limited, helpless—he is no longer "supreme" (1 Pet. iii:13); there is something above him. Of what use is it to have a large fortune if we cannot spend it? Of what use to be rich in mercy if one cannot exercise it? Of what use to be a King if one cannot show that quality of benevolence: mercy. *"The Throne is upholden by mercy."*

So put the two passages in Proverbs together and we learn that righteousness is the only foundation for a throne; mercy its only support. And if this is true of an earthly throne; much more must it be true of the Throne of God.

There must therefore be no lack of either righteousness on the one hand, or mercy on the other, for the integrity and maintenance of the Throne of God. Now we may see why Satan ever seeks to drag his victims before the Throne as criminals. If there be an inability to show *mercy*— one speaks with all reverence—God's very throne is of no value to Him. If He is powerless to save those He loves, and wills to bless, of what good is His Throne? It lacks power—strength to carry out His will, and He is no longer supreme. But if He pardons convicted criminals—is that righteous? Is not the foundation gone? If He cannot pardon, where is the mercy? If He does, where is the righteousness? It is ever Satan's subtle way to place in a dilemma; and this is a dilemma worthy of being put even before God. Apparently there is no escape for, whichever horn of the dilemma be accepted, the Throne—that Throne he was appointed to guard is subverted; and since he would himself be as God, *why does not that subversion place it at his own command?*

But now with these Scriptures in mind, turn to another illustration, and a very clear and striking one it is, worthy of our most careful attention. You will find it in the 6th chap. of Daniel. There we are told that the Persian King, Darius, had exalted a poor captive "over all the presidents and princes of his Kingdom." Can we not enter into the situation? These princes had hitherto been

unrivalled in their dignities, and now one far below them in social condition is put above them.
Do we not see the parallel? This was exactly the
state of affairs when Adam, taken from the dust,
was set over the kingdom over which Satan a
glorious spirit, had hitherto been unrivalled. Well,
the Persian princes conceive a plan whereby they
may strike a blow that shall at once satisfy their
malice against the King, get rid of Daniel, and
secure their own authority forever; and this all
based (mark it well) on the tender love of the
King for Daniel: exactly paralleling Satan's plans
against God by means of the tenderly-loved man.

Having arranged the plot they approach the
King with one of those lies that is covered with
enough truth to show its real author: *"King
Darius live forever. All the presidents of the
Kingdom, and the princes, the counsellors, and the
captains, have consulted together to establish a
royal statute, and to make a firm decree, that whosoever shall ask a petition of any god or man for
thirty days, save of thee, O King, he shall be cast
into the den of lions."*

Note the natural effect of this on Darius—*"All*
the presidents," he would say to himself, "then my
beloved Daniel is also in favor of this decree; and
it certainly is a very attractive thought that for a
time at least I shall be in the place of all that
is divine: it shows great consideration for my
honor on the part of my presidents and princes"—

HIS MOTIVE.

It was an excellent trap, well baited, and the unsuspecting King walks in, signs the decree, the spring snaps behind him, and he is taken.

Like all trapped creatures, he tries to get out. He desires with all his heart to have mercy on his beloved Daniel, and "labors till the going down of the sun" to deliver him. He wants to exercise that support, or comfort, the prerogative of the throne: mercy; and especially to one who has only broken a wicked law.

But it is impossible. He cannot be both a just King in maintaining his own laws, and a Saviour too. He might as well be the poorest of his subjects as far as any power of carrying out his will goes. He is a helpless King, on an impotent Throne—a picture of *Love powerless against Law*.

Now turn to a scene in which every factor that we have been looking at in this Persian Court is reproduced, but in infinitely stronger colors.

Turn to John viii, and you will find an incident there recorded that, according to the weight of modern biblical criticism should not be in our Bibles at all; but according to any spiritual intelligence it gives such marks of the Finger of God, that it could not be anywhere else.

For no holy man is here condemned by a flagrantly unrighteous law; but a sinner so hopelessly guilty that she has not one word to say in self defense. No heathen princes press for judgment, but all the religious heads of the community, who remind the

Lord Jesus of the unequivocal words "Moses in the
law" had written regarding the disposition of such
a case, and then they add "but what sayest thou?"

And in Him we have another contrast, for
He is no Darius. He stoops down and writes
with His finger in the dust, and they—poor, foolish
men, like Belshazzar of old—cannot read His writing. They continue to press their supposed advantage, "Moses indeed said that she should be stoned;
now can you, the pretended Messiah, be *just* and be
a *Saviour,* too?"

Daniel was guiltless, yet the King could not save
him in opposition to an unjust, wicked human law;
here is a hopelessly guilty one; can He save such
in view of a holy, just, good divine law? If He
says "Stone her" then is He no Saviour and cannot
show mercy; if He says "Stone her not" then is He
unjust?

It is a deeper problem than that of the tribute
money. It is the one mighty problem of the ages,
a problem that God alone can ever solve; therefore
is it placed with beautiful exactness in this gospel of
His divine glory; and His solution of it marks Him
absolutely divine.

He continues to write with His finger on the
ground. What sentence was that finger writing?
What sentence had that same divine Finger written
long, long ago? Had it not even in Eden written
to one sinning head of the sinful race, "Dust thou
art." It was the same here, that Finger was *tracing*

*in that common dust from which all came, to which
all returned, a common sin, a common condemnation.*
The very dust touched by His Finger answered this
question. But what message does it carry to the
hearts and consciences of the hearers? They read it
not; till, lifting Himself up, He tells them plainly,
"He that is without sin among you, let him cast the
first stone." It is the same thing as He wrote in
Eden, as He had just written in that dust. A common sin, a common condemnation, under which all
alike lay. Well, do they cast stones? No, they go
out, beginning at the oldest. Convicted by their own
consciences, they leave His Presence and leave the
poor silent sinner there alone—alone with Him who
could alone indeed cast the first stone—But what
does He do? He lifts up Himself, and no con-
demner left, says "Neither do I condemn thee; go,
and sin no more." The Cross shall soon prove Him
righteous in so speaking, for the stones shall fall on
Him for the sin then "passed over." Here one sees
Law powerless against Love.

Now leaving many points of exquisite beauty in
the narrative let me ask with all earnestness, do you
think that it was any consideration of public policy
or care for public morality, that governed those men
in bringing that woman before Christ? Or that, in
so doing *they arrived at her at all?* Consider it well,
Did they aim at her? Most certainly not: for had
that been their motive, there would have been no
need to bring her there at all: the law was clear,

there were plenty of stones, and willing hands to throw them. *No, they could only be aiming at Him.* And when, in that sphere, of which we are bold to say this is a divinely intended picture, the great arch-enemy brings sinful man before the judgment seat, he *does not aim at the man at all but at the Judge; not at the guilty sinner but at God.*

As a further justification for looking upon the scene as pictorial or symbolical, note that it is in this very chapter that He charges these very men with doing *"the deeds of their father the Devil"* v.40. It is exactly what they were doing even then: they, in a small scale, what *he* is ever doing in a larger one.

These incidents then furnish illustrations strongly confirmatory of all that we have gathered as to Satan's motive in his work with man: it is not else or less than to subvert and acquire the Throne of God.

CHAPTER XVII.

THE CHRISTIAN'S CONFLICT.

Contents.

We have thus considered the *character* of the Devil's work with man; the motive for it; and glanced, all too briefly, at the way God in His Love and Wisdom turns all to the blessing of His creatures, both in heaven and earth, by revealing to them both "the exceeding riches of His grace" and His "manifold wisdom" in meeting the craft of the great enemy.

But I may not close this part of our subject without some reference to the Christian's present conflict with the Devil, and the hosts of subordinate, but mighty spirits under him called "principalities and powers" and "wicked spirits" in Ephesians vi., and the provision the same Lord in His wisdom has made for our present victory in this conflict.

Scripture has, I trust, made it quite clear that each part of our being: spirit, soul and body, has its own peculiar enemy. The body is opposed to, and in constant danger of being brought under bondage to that evil principle within it, *the flesh*. The soul finds its peculiar opponent in the *world;* whilst the spirit naturally, and reasonably, is in conflict with that evil spirit: the Devil. Spirit, soul and body are thus opposed by Devil, world and flesh, each to each. Further, this Trinity of evil is equally clearly opposed to the divine Trinity: Father, Son and Holy Spirit. The world opposed to the Father, as 1 John ii:15 teaches us: *"if any man love the world, the love of the Father is not in him."* The Devil opposed to the Son, as all through the Scriptures. The flesh opposed to the Spirit, as Gal. v:16, 17 clearly teaches *"Walk in the Spirit, and ye shall not fulfill the lust of the flesh. For the flesh lusteth against the Spirit, and the Spirit against the flesh, and these are contrary the one to the other."*

Now, world, flesh and Devil are very closely united, so that it may at times be difficult to distinguish one from another; the last using the two former for his purposes; but, to this, that word that separates between soul and spirit (Heb. iv), will help us.

Let us glance at each, and the way God's word instructs us to deal with it; for each is to be dealt with, according to the light of the Word of God, not our thought. First as to the flesh—what is it? It is *not* the body, for that is to be sanctified, and at all times "worthy of a certain degree of honor" (as a correct reading of Col. ii:23 teaches), as the Temple of the Holy Ghost. The recluses, and asceties of the middle ages hoped by inflicting blows on the poor body to reach "the flesh"; but ever failed. Nay, fleshly pride may become very vigorous under each treatment. Yet is the flesh not altogether disconnected from the body, for this is the sphere, or field, in which it has its way. The "flesh" is the *nature of the first man, fallen from God,* and its will, or mind, is *"enmity with God,"* and can never be anything else: *"not subject to the law of God, neither indeed can be"* (Rom. viii:7).

Deliverance from its power is not obtained according to God, by fighting it. It is not to be *resisted;* but to be turned from. Every occasion that would incite it is to be avoided. See how consistently this is taught: *"Flee youthful lusts"* (2 Tim. ii:22). *"Abstain, or keep away from fleshly lusts"* (1 Pet. ii:11). *Flee fornication* (1 Cor. vi). Amongst Israel's foes, it was represented by Edom who was not to be fought, but (as Peter teaches) also turned away from, see Num. xx:21. "Desires" can only be overcome "by the expulsive power of a new affection." The only way that any can stop coveting evil is to have something better before one. In Rom. vii we see a picture of a struggle against the flesh; but it is the bootless struggle of a helpless captive, not the conflict of an armed warrior. We must go to Rom. viii:2 for the secret of victory: not by struggle; but by turning away: the *"law of the Spirit"* turns me to find my *"life in Christ Jesus,"* and this is the way of freedom from the law of sin and death.

As to the *"world,"* we must similarly clearly distinguish it from the *earth,* or nature. Neither the earth, nor the beauties it contains, are to be avoided, but enjoyed in communion with God. The *"world"* is the present system of things, morally, politically, religiously, away from God. The scriptures exhort us—not to "fight", as could only be done with carnal weapons; not to "flee from," nor get out of it literally; but to "be not conformed" to it (Rom. xii), not to "love" it (1 John ii) not to be "a friend" with it (James iv) all negatives; as if we were to have nothing to do with it. It is opposed to the Father, the blessed Home Name, and relationship of God. If I know God as my Father, and what that involves, the world loses its power to detain me, I must be getting Home. It is the Son who thus reveals the Father (Matt. xi), and faith in Jesus as the Son of God, overcomes the world (1 John v:4). It is ruled by the Devil, its prince, who governs it in morals, in politics, and in religion. It is perfectly adapted to the flesh; but the child of God passes through it (does not flee from it however), a stranger and a pilgrim, with heart longing for a better home.

But we are more concerned with the third enemy, the Devil, who must be met in stern conflict face to

face. Far from the divine counsel being flight, it is
"fight." Again and again, we are told to "*resist* the
Devil," with a cheering promise added that in that
case *he* will be the one that flees (James iv:7), and
that, not because of any superior power of our
own; but because he is a conquered foe, and our
Lord Jesus Christ is his conqueror, and we are His.

But may we get more clearly defined what are
the varying characters of his attacks, and what
therefore is necessary for a successful resistance?

The nature of these may clearly and certainly be
gathered from his own present nature as Scripture
reveals it. As he is a liar and a murderer, so will
he use both corruption and violence to attain his
ends. So did he act through Balaam and Balak.
First he tried violence in the cursing; but God
turned his curses into blessings. Then he turned to
corruption; and was far more successful for a time
at least, as the fair daughters of Moab caused the
host to forget their pilgrimage. Exactly thus has
he acted with the heavenly pilgrim, the church.
In the days of Smyrna (Rev. ii:8-11) he tried
"violence," in persecution; but the Lord again
turned it to blessing. Then in Pergamos he changed
his tactics, and once more teaches the same doctrine
as Balaam taught Balak; and once more with far
greater success, for from that moment the church
forgets her *pilgrim* character, and dwells where
Satan's throne is, and where he dwells. (Rev. ii:13)
they share one home.

So he comes against individuals, either as a "roaring lion" (1 Pet. v), or with the "wiles" of the *serpent* (Eph. vi).

But whether he uses this weapon or that, his aim is ever the same: to get away man's heart, his love and confidence away from God. For not only is the *earth* the object of the strife between the Lord Jesus and the Devil, as to who shall be its King; but the man upon it—who shall have his heart's confidence, who shall really be his *God?* The Devil claims both the earth and the man; the Lord Jesus has a counter-claim.

This then suggests very clearly the root-aim of his attacks: it is always to destroy faith in God; and our side of the conflict is to maintain that faith in spite of anything he can bring against it. So the apostle Peter says whom resist *steadfast* in the *faith;* and our own apostle's joyful swan-song is: *"I have fought a good fight I have finished the course, I have kept the faith"*; and he passes back the word to us "fight the good fight of *faith*" (1 Tim. vi:12).

Perhaps we may think that not often does he make use of violence in his attacks in these days; and yet it may be questioned if this is not far more frequent than would justify such thoughts. If violence, or persecution, is limited to martyrdom by wild beast, fire, or sword; then, clearly since these have in large measure passed away, at least from the so-called civilized world, his violence is gone too. But not thus do the Scriptures speak; and I venture to say not thus does our experience witness. It is plainly written that *"he that was born after the flesh* (Ishmael) *persecuted him born after the spirit* (Isaac). But how? Did he torture or slay the child? Not at all; he simply *mocked* (Gen. xxi:9). God calls mockery: the sneer, the jest—persecution. Do we never feel it, and shrink from it, and often escape it at great cost? Is there no one that mocks you in all your environment at home or abroad? Again, the Lord Jesus pronounced blessed those persecuted, aye, but more: *"blessed are ye when men shall revile you,"* the reviling you see is on the same level as persecution. Again allow me to ask have you and I *never* felt the edge of this weapon? In workshop, in office, in mart, in home are the Lord's people constantly tempted to deny their allegiance to the Lord Jesus through the fear of this form of violence.

But more successful as more subtle is the other force and a myriad of opportunities does our enemy find to use it. We are passing through *his* country, under his government still, and how constantly he uses that fact to distress and perplex the people of God. He points to adverse providence, to earth-quakes, floods, fires, and their consequences (in all of which he may have a much more active part than we have thought), and suggests "would God permit that, if He loved or cared?"

In the black hour of sorrow too, when all the broken heart-strings of the bereaved fly back and

SATAN.

cause unspeakable anguish; ah! then his hosts often gather around the sufferer, till they shut out all light; and, in the solitude of that darkness, he hears only the wild hellish suggestions of questions as to God's love; nay, often, as to His very being: is there really a God, a heaven, a hell, or is all summed up in what I see—cold, heartless, unsympathetic matter, and time and chance happening alike to all (Eccles. ix :ii)? At such times existence seems like a terrible machine made up of eccentric wheels, that work without any regularity, into which poor man is thrust at birth; and sooner or later pitilessly ground out again at death, without a particle of sympathy, or apparently intelligence: Time and Doom governing everything!

Nor is the Devil confined to this shady side of life's pathway, he can equally use the sunny; and argue from material prosperity, and the so-called progress, due to human skill and ingenuity, that the earth is getting on very well under *his* rule; nor does it need the return of the Lord Jesus to put things in order. In this he is very successful.

Much more might be said, but we must pause and turn to the weapons divinely granted us to use against him.

CHAPTER XVIII.

THE WHOLE ARMOR OF GOD.

Contents.

The panoply: put it on.—The foe.—Its various parts.

God be thanked we have a complete suit of armor divinely provided for our conflict with the Devil and his hosts and we may look at it in Eph. vi: verses 11 to 18. We will read together.

Put on the panoply of God that ye may be able to stand against the wiles of the devil.

Put on no other armor; but be very careful to put on *this;* and the *whole* of it; and keep it on; for your mighty enemy's attacks are not once for all, but constantly recurring. The word for "wiles" *methodeias* (English: methods") combines both craft and power. He knows the best weapons to employ; the weakest side to attack; the favorable moment for delivering the attack. Unless one has a due sense of the almost infinite superiority of the Devil in natural capacity, in skill, in cunning, we shall lack a due sense of our need, and fail to put on the panoply: so the power of the foe is now defined.

Because our wrestling is not against blood and

flesh (where there would be some equality) *but against the principalities* (chiefs; not inferior spirits only, but the actual leaders of the various groups of the rebellious spirits) *against the authorities* (the commanders whose combined counsels may direct the assault) *against the world-rulers of this darkness* (the word *world-rulers* suggests the sphere and limits of the authority: *this darkness* the ethical character of their realm as away from God: Light. Satan being Prince of this world, his angels under him are *world-rulers,* but only in the sense of the world having departed from God, therefore *"of this darkness, against the spiritual (powers) of wickedness* (practically, "wicked spirits") *in the heavenlies.*

It is the antitype of the conflict in the book of Joshua. We are here seen as beyond death (Jordan) and in the land or "heavenly places" where we are opposed, not as was Israel, by blood and flesh; but by the mightiest of wicked spirits; who as the Canaanite nations, still hold possession of our inheritance, and would prevent our enjoyment of it. It is in the heavenlies where are all our blessings, and in which, in some real sense, Christians are: the term must therefore have, as do all this group of words, an ethical, spiritual, or moral bearing, not physical, as above the stars, but of highest spiritual privilege. The "Kingdom of the heavens" is on earth; but the heavenlies themselves are not at all of earth, but spiritual.

THE CHRISTIAN ARMOR.

Because of this, take up (a technical expression, as we say "take up arms") *the panoply of God, that ye may be able to withstand in the evil day* (*i. e.,* those times of special conflict and trial that occur in all lives from time to time), *and having done all to stand.* When a *battle* is over; the war is not; and a feigned retreat is often a successful ruse; so, after each struggle, we must stand prepared for the next. The poor man of God who came out of Judah fought a splendid fight of faith; but he failed to "stand": sat down under the oak, and the lion killed him. Ah, there is no release in this war, till He come. But now for the armor.

Stand therefore having your loins girt about with truth. The girdle braces up, or sustains the whole man. And beautifully has Truth the first place in the armor of God. I must *know* that what I am resting on is really true, or how can I withstand any attack on that resting place? If there is the slightest uncertainty as to this, I am proportionately weak. Mark, it is *Truth,* not *facts,* not history; for those may, and do, leave out God: Truth never does. *The* Liar, beyond all others, is not one who twists, or distorts, or denies facts, but denies "Jesus is the Christ," (1 John ii:22). The *Truth* then is inclusive of all God's revelation to men; and one might as soon expect to get a sum of addition correct whilst leaving out the largest item, as to think one has "the Truth" without God or His dear Son. To-day all Truth is attacked by Satan, and his subtle darts fly thick on every hand.

SATAN.

All that has been accepted in the past as sure and certain is questioned; or a crafty doubt suggested to the mind that may serve to shake it. "Is the Bible God's revelation to man? Look at the difficulties in it; mark its many obscurities; can it be divine? How can Christ be the Eternal Son of God? Is not a Father necessarily before a Son? How then *Eternal?* Can you believe in the paradoxes of Christianity, such as a Triune God; the birth from a virgin, and such extravagances? Do you not know that all thoughtful people have given them up, with the exploded teachings as to hell, the Devil, a literal resurrection, and a coming again at any hour, or any moment of any hour?" Well, we must just face these things, not flee from them one inch, and yet it is just from these that Christians do flee—reversing the divine directions. They are the very Girdle of Truth. God does not ask us to believe absurdities, or anything contrary to the reason He has given; but as surely as your baby believes you, without being able to understand all you say; so surely there must be much *beyond* our reason in God's revelation, or we might fairly reject it as divine. Be quite sure that you have *the truth;* then put it on as a girdle and let nothing in the heavenlies or on earth, pull it off.

> Let all the forms that men devise
>   Assault my soul with treacherous art,
> I'll call them vanity and lies,
>   And bind thy Gospel to my heart.

THE CHRISTIAN ARMOR.

And having put on the breast plate of righteousness. That is the external consequence of truth in life: the practical walk in accord with the truth held. This is a very weak spot with many of us to-day. We have much truth; but how little does conduct correspond with it. This makes us very vulnerable in the *breast;* for our *affections* become sadly chilled. It may be truthfully said that never, since the days of the apostles, was as much truth known as amongst certain circles of Christians to-day, but are they as devoted, as unworldly, as tender in affection to every fellow saint, as heavenly minded— we will not say, as the apostles, but—as even those true saints who lived in the darkest ages, and of whom Mrs. Bevan tells us in her "Three Friends of God?" Alas, are not many of us "holding truth in unrighteousness?" What must be the consequence? Oh beloved, there is the loudest call for repentance here.

And the feet shod with the preparation of the gospel of peace. This is the foot armor, making one always ready and alert for what may come; for unless properly shod, one can neither stand securely, walk easily, or fight victoriously. For this, *peace* is of the first necessity. The Israelites in Egypt were not fighters but slaves. The Passover was to them, "the gospel of peace"; and they ate it with shoes on their feet: shoes that, as a figure, were never put off for they never "waxed old"; and with them they were always prepared to "stand still," or to "go

forward" (Ex. xiv :8), or to "fight" (Ex. xiv :9).
It is to be feared that many pilgrims to-day
are so poor that they walk, or rather crawl,
barefoot. Note peace is a preparedness for
war. If one is not at peace with God he is not "prepared" for anything. He cannot wrestle with spiritual foes if he has any question as to his relations
with God. I must know God loves me ; I must know
death and judgment are behind me forever ; and this
means peace in the heart and conscience. I must
know it, for it is the very thing the darts of the
wicked are aimed at : my heart's rest in God. These
shoes give a very springy step, and are always a
perfect fit to our condition.

And as a divinely given illustration of these
"shoes" let me remind you once more of those the
Israelites had on when leaving Egypt—they "waxed
not old." That is, they were the same shoes all
through their journeying. But did not the feet at
least of the younger pilgrims *grow?* Must they not
then have been greatly discomforted by these
"shoes?" Certainly they would if the shoes had not
also expanded. But without in the least pressing
such literal details there can be no question that the
whole narrative compels us to assert of the antitype; "the preparation of the Gospel of peace"—
that shoes made of this material *do* expand as the
wearers grow. There are some Christians who do
not think the shoes do expand, and they just remain
at the most fundamental and primary truths of the

gospel all their lives. They never enjoy the deep things of God. There are others who think that *they* have outgrown the shoes; and they look down on these Gospel truths as milk for babes. Both are quite wrong. The Gospel grows as we grow. We grow, and find greater depth, greater breadth, greater length in the Gospel to meet the greater *need,* (not greater *attainment,* mind), we find in ourselves. We neither outgrow the shoes; nor remain at one stay—they are always a perfect fit to our changing conditions.

In addition to all these take the shield of faith, wherewith ye shall be able to quench all the burning darts of the wicked one.

The wicked one is that particular spiritual foe that makes the attack; but as he acts *for* the Devil, it may be applied to the Devil himself. He throws darts that are fire-tipped; causing, if not caught on the shield, intense pain. Job so caught them when he said *"the Lord gave, the Lord hath taken away, blessed be the name of the Lord."* Days of sorrow are peculiarly favorable for these darts; where circumstances appear to confirm the awful suggestion that God does not love or care for us at all. Oh for the shield of faith; of such knowledge of Him, and His love, seen in the cross of His dear Son, as renders null all these efforts of the enemy. Whenever you are tempted by untoward circumstances to doubt God's love to you my reader, ask yourself two questions: Who hung on that central cross?

Why was He there? You will find the shield of
faith catches the doubt.

And receive the helmet of salvation, "receive"
as if God Himself were handing us this, and all that
were needed is just to take it. When it comes to
salvation, all we can do is always just to *"take"*.
So the saints of God have ever found, through all
dispensations, as harken to David—in Ps. cxvi:12—
*"What shall I render unto the Lord for all His
benefits towards me."* And he answers his question,
"The best return I can think of, knowing how *giving* refreshes and delights Him, how my receiving
honors Him, is to *"take the cup of salvation"* and
still continue to *"call on the Name of the Lord."*
This "helmet of salvation" sets very comfortably on
the head. Many people seem to think that this
piece of armor belongs to the *heart*: that is, they
make salvation a question of *feeling*. No, no, put it
on the *head,* which surely stands for the intelligence,
the reason, the conscience; and you will find it very
light, and indeed bringing a kind of sunshine with
it, that is very distressing to the world-rulers of
"this darkness;" for they hate to see anyone joying
in God's salvation. Never mind, we are not putting
on this armor to please them.

But we must have an offensive weapon too, and
here it is:

*"And the sword of the Spirit which is the word
(or rather 'saying') of God."* This also is just to be
"taken." Divine love has provided it, and put it

into our hands. Yes, we must carefully note that it is not the Sword of the *flesh,* but of the Spirit. The first man must not touch it, or he will be cutting the wrong people. In how many of the wretched contentions between saints has this Sword been thus used carefully? In a figure, Samson so wielded it, when he caught those 300 foxes and tied torches to the tails of each pair; for the only result was the destruction of corn, vines and olives. What was there of blessing to Israel in that? And when flesh uses this Sword it is always destructive to everything that feeds, comforts or edifies the Lord's people. The Spirit of God alone knows how to wield it; when, and against whom to apply it. Then again, note, it is not exactly the *Word of God as a whole,* but that particular word, or saying, that shall be just adapted to the occasion. Apart from the Spirit, even the most intelligent of Christians are very apt to misapply Scripture, and get quite a wrong word for the occasion. There is some "saying of God" to meet every crisis, every attack of the wicked one; and the Holy Spirit alone can direct us to it; but He will, if we do not grieve Him.

But still there is one other piece of armor—a strange one—it is called "all prayer"—

"Praying always with all prayer and supplication in the Spirit."

This is a very necessary weapon, and very effective, for

> "Satan trembles when he sees,
> The weakest saint upon his knees."

Note the *"always,"* literally *"in every season."*
This weapon must be at hand, in prosperity as well
as in adversity; in joy as well as in sorrow; in health
as well as sickness; in the smiles of the world as
well as in its frowns; in gain as well as in loss; in
rest as well as in activity; in business as well
as in the home. Every state, every season,
every place, has its own peculiar dangers.
So prayer is needed in all. But not only this,
or because of this, it is *"all* prayer"; that
is, the diverse needs give occasion for diverse
prayers. When you always go through about the
same form of words in prayer, it is greatly to be
feared that you are simply in a rut, and not realiz-
ing the peculiar needs of that moment. Your prayer
is a form—you are "saying your prayers"; or as is
the hateful expression, "making a prayer." Did
Peter "say his prayers" when the water was going
over him? No, indeed. But further: "supplication"
is added. Is not this simply tautology? What is
supplication if not prayer? Prayer is to be "without
ceasing"; but supplication is for *times of special
pressure.* Some specific need or lack is pressed
upon us, and this leads to *supplication. Prayer* is
the general spirit of dependence; *supplication* meets
special needs. If I might so put it, prayer brings me
to my knees, supplication throws me on my face.

Now, my beloved brother or sister, let us press
upon our souls the need of practical use of this
armor. It is not like those antiquated suits we are

accustomed to look at with curiosity in the Tower of London, or elsewhere; it is for *present* use, and has never been improved upon. Modern weapons are out of date in a few years—this armor, never. God does not tell us to look at it, to admire it, but to put it on; for armor is not one atom of use until it is put on.

By the unspeakable superiority of our foes in strength and skill: by our own weakness and folly: by our past experience of failure and fall: by the weighty issues at stake: by the seriousness of the conflict: by the near approach of everlasting deliverance: by the goodness of God in making the provision; by the love of Christ and His honor which we carry, let us see to it that by the same grace that gave, we "put on the *whole* armor of God."

CHAPTER XIX.

THE DEVIL'S POWER OF DEATH.

Contents.

How has the Devil the power of Death?—Are saints or sinners in view in Heb. ii:14?—The O. T. saints view of Death.—The reasonableness of such fear of Death.— Illustration.

In this connection we may look at a remarkable expression in Hebrews ii:14, which suggests a further phase of the Devil's work amongst men. *"Forasmuch then as the children are partakers of flesh and blood, he also himself likewise took part of the same; that through death he might destroy him who had the power of death, that is, the devil; and deliver them who through fear of death were all their lifetime subject to bondage."*

The question naturally arises, how can the Devil have, or ever have had "the power of death?" Does it mean that he actually has been, and is the agent— a kind of executioner—in carrying out the divine sentence *"thou shalt surely die;"* and that thus the whole race, not merely owes that first death-sentence to him; but that each individual is literally brought to the dust by his direct agency?

THE POWER OF DEATH.

Such a thought would need much clearer Scripture for its support than any questionable deduction from this verse; nor will either the context, nor the word used for "power"—which has in it, not the idea of authority, but strength—permit it. The Devil has been actually "destroyed" by the death of Him who partook of flesh and blood. But how? He is not dead; and Death still reigns over the bodies of all men, believer as well as unbeliever. There is doubtless a mighty difference between them, it is *not* in the saint's escape from death. "If Christ be in you, what is the consequence? Is the body affected by that fact yet." No, *"the body is indeed dead because of sin:"* that is, the body is not yet redeemed by power from the consequences of sin. Death still has its claims upon it. You cannot say because Christ is in you that your body is in resurrection life, since it is exactly for this that we still wait (v. 23). What then is the distinctive result of Christ being in you? *"The Spirit is life because of righteousness."* The Holy Spirit, as giving divine life to my spirit, is life: life never to be touched by death. And why? Because death has lost all power over this Spirit-given, Spirit-filled life. How? *"Because of righteousness"* that has put away all that called for death in the One who died in the likeness of sinful flesh on the Cross. We shall, *as to the spirit "never see death"* (John viii:51).

This then gives its light to our Scripture in Heb.

SATAN.

ii. From what has the blessed Saviour delivered His people, since not from actual death? From that *fear of death* which is its power, and which the Devil has ever wielded against His people; bringing them into bondage.

But of whom is the inspired writer of Hebrews speaking? Is it the race of mankind as a whole, or the "sons" God is "bringing to glory?" Beyond any question it is the latter, not the whole race. It is the children of God, who, all through past ages, have, through fear of death, been subject to bondage.

As to men at large, with conscience falsely soothed, if not seared, they may certainly at times have spasms of terror, as the certainty and awfulness of death forces itself upon them. Perhaps the wretched criminal, condemned to execution in the prime of manhood and vigor of health, may collapse with great fear. Perhaps now and again, in the darkness of the night, when sleep refuses to come, the dread "Beyond" with all its possibilities and uncertainties, may make death to be, even to all (to you, my reader?) the King of Terrors. But as a rule, it is not the man of the world who fears death. Nay, he frequently makes his freedom from that fear a distinct boast; but it is only because be is insensible to what it involves. When the spirit is awakened, when eternal realities press upon us, when alarmed conscience accuses, when its witness to guilt is accepted—in a word when the man is a *quickened* soul, as were O. T. saints, but with no knowledge of the perfection of redemption already and forever effected, then is there still the fear of Death, as there ever was.

Apart from this action of the Spirit of God, men are "as the beasts that perish" as Ps. xlix speaks, that is, the part of their being that alone distinguishes them from the irrational beasts is *dead* towards God and they no more fear death than does the dog or horse. They are on one level with them in this respect: and they boast of it!

He is writing then of the "children of God" of all the time prior to the Lord's atoning death, not of men at large, for this phenomenon of the insensate character of men at large was one of the perplexities of Asaph: *"They have no bands in their death"* he sighed in Ps. lxxiii., which does not mean that they have an easy death, without pain; but their death does not throw its shadow over their life, they do not realize what it means; it does not bring them into "bands" or bondage. They do not fear it .

But let us listen to what the Lord's people thought of Death: *"Cease then and let me alone, that I may take comfort a little, before I go whence I shall not return, even to the land of darkness, as darkness itself, and of the shadow of death, without any order, and whose light is as darkness."* Oh, think of one esteeming Death to be the entering a land of such darkness that its very daylight is midnight darkness. Can you wonder that there was **"fear"**?

SATAN.

But hearken again. Heman the Ezrahite sings:
*"Wilt thou show wonders to the dead? Shall the
dead arise and praise thee? Shall thy loving kindness be declared in the grave, or thy faithfulness
in destruction? Shall thy wonders be known in the
dark? And thy righteousness in the land of forgetfulness?"* Ps. lxxxviii. Is it to be wondered at
that people shrank with terror from such a condition?

Once more to the psalmist it is a land of gloomy
silence for *"the dead praise not the Lord, nor any
that go down into silence."* Ps. cxv:17.

And would you learn the views of death arrived
at in that day by the wisest of all men, then hear
Solomon declare that *"a living dog is better than
a dead lion. For the living know that they shall
die* (1 Cor. xv:51 was unknown *then*), *but the dead
know not anything; neither have they any more a
reward, for the memory of them is forgotten. Also
their love, and their hatred, and their envy is now
perished; neither have they any more a portion forever, in anything that is done under the sun."* Ecc.
ix:5, 6.

Solomon is of course dealing solely with what
may be seen "under the sun"; as far as mere
unaided human wisdom can discern. That the pious
Israelite looked upon death as the cessation of existence is absolutely disproved from all Scripture.
The Lord's words as to the rich man and Lazarus
did not clash, in this respect, with what was uni-

versally held, except by those "rationalists" or annihilationists of that day; the Sadducees and He confounds these in Matt. xxii:23 to 32.

Indeed the fact that death is not *the end* is, or was, the very cause of its terror; and it was the quickened, not *dead,* spirit that realized this. We may count it amongst one of the multitude of proofs of the divinity of the Scriptures that they, of all writings, speak of the fear of death as being a characteristic of the true saint in a certain condition, rather than of the lost sinner. Let a man consider its *certainty*—not a possibility of escape (speaking normally, and omitting the mystery of 1 Cor. xv.) it lies before every one that breathes, in more or less proximity: let him think of the pain and suffering that usually lead up to it; the *sorrow* and anguish of those bereaved; the strange, new, untried conditions into which it introduces, sending the conscious part of man's being into a scene where he is more helpless than when, as a babe, he was first thrown into this world; the *dark, dark cloud* that hangs over that "beyond" as it is called; but above all, let him remember his wasted years, his myriad sins, his defiance of God and His law, his grievous and repeated moral lapses from light and love, and then let him remember too that *"it is appointed unto men once to die but after this the judgment,"* and that *"everyone of us shall give account of himself to God,"* and surely fear is the only evidence of *sanity* or of reason being in its place. He who can go out of life without fear, is either perfectly sinless, or a madman, or has learned some secret more precious than rubies, for, after all, the sting of death is not its certainty, its pain, its sorrow, its strange conditions, but *Sin* 1 Cor. xv.

But whilst then fear is exactly fitting, and indeed necessary *before* the death and resurrection of the Lord Jesus, has that stupendous fact effected no change in these conditions? Indeed it has—it has removed the cause of the fear; it has not put away its pain, or sorrow, or strange conditions; but it has put away its *sting,* and has delivered from all bondage, and destroyed the Devil.

But how is this: granting that sin gives death its power, how does this connect it with the Devil, or put that power into his hands? In one way only; (and th:s gives a further confirmation of Ezek. xviii). As exercising his office of *"cherub that covereth,"* in accusing. Let me illustrate: I am in prison under a capital charge; one only can give testimony at my coming trial that shall surely secure my condemnation, and this one is also the Prosecuting District Attorney, who is bound by his office to see that the righteousness of the government is maintained and justice done. Every day he visits me in my cell to assure me that he will press the case, and to convince me of its hopelessness. Oh, the bondage of my spirit, as well as of my body. I know not what joyous liberty of mind or body is,

THE POWER OF DEATH.

I am in constant fear of death; and the Attorney has the *power* of it. One day a well-known man of stainless integrity and unimpeachable veracity visits my cell with these strange tidings: "your case has been settled; you have indeed been 'condemned already' as guilty, but one who dearly loves you has voluntarily assumed your place, has been willingly accepted as a substitute by the authorities, and his body even now swings on the gallows in the prison yard; and if you will willingly accept him as your substitute, you are free." If I believe the tidings am I not delivered? Do I now fear that stern attorney and malicious witness at all? Am I affected now by his threats? How much of his *power* is left him? It is altogether gone. He is, as an accuser, *"destroyed"*; I snap my fingers in his face.

The illustration may be defective but it will serve, for just thus "through death" has our Lord Jesus brought to nothing all the accuser's power; and according to the simplicity of our faith in the glad-tidings proclaimed "with the Holy Ghost sent down from heaven," will be our deliverance from the fear of death.

Still Satan poses as an angel of light; that is, as one who desires only to maintain righteousness, and still he presses on the conscience that righteousness surely demands eternal condemnation. Oh, happy beyond expression is the poorest, and simplest, yea guiltiest, who knows that, not mercy (although this is the basis of all) but righteousness—strict *righteousness,* even the *righteousness of God* demands and necessitates, not his condemnation, but justification; and the Devil cannot utter one word of protest. He is "annulled," "destroyed"—will you not at least say with me, Thanks be unto God who giveth us the victory through our Lord Jesus Christ, forever and forever.

CHAPTER XX.

THE CHRISTIAN VIEW OF DEATH.

Contents.

In continuation of this subject, let us see the normal Christian view of Death. There are those who teach us that no further light has been granted us on this theme than that attained by the wisest of men, who, seeing both men and beasts die, could not discern any difference. In both cases heart ceased to beat, pulse to throb, and lungs to breathe. As far as he could see they had "all one breath," and who could tell whether it went up or down, so that "a man hath no pre-eminence above a beast," Ecc. iii:19-21: and this, we are told by certain modern Doctors of Divinity, is the measure of divine revelation even to this day. Still man dies as the beast dies; still, if not an actual cessation of existence, Death is at least and at best, an un-

conscious dreamless sleep, from which the last
trump alone shall ever waken the sleepers.

We have already seen many evidences of the fear
of Death, and subsequent bondage of those who
had this light (or darkness) and this only: are we
in the same case?

Then for us too the death condition is but "the
land of forgetfulness," "of darkness as darkness
itself, where the light is as darkness"; it is going
"down into silence"; where there is no knowledge,
no joy, no praise—*nothing*? If that be true; then,
let men say what they will, the "fear of Death" is
not altogether taken away. Even a joyous resurrection, either far off or near, will never make
unconsciousness to be preferred to the conscious
enjoyment of life, its activities and powers. People
do not take anaesthetics normally as a matter of
pleasure, nor because it is "far better."

But no, blessed be God, a flood of beauteous
light has poured into the tomb since Solomon's
day; and as we look into one empty grave never
more to be filled, we raise our hearts in song, for
*He "hath abolished Death and brought life and
incorruptibility to light through the gospel";* that
gospel that was never heard till Jesus was with the
Father.

"Abolished Death!" do not many of us exclaim
"would that it were abolished, and that nevermore
should human tears be shed over human dead; but
is not Death as active to-day as ever; how then

abolished?" Exactly as we have seen the Devil *destroyed,* for the word is the same in both cases; nor in either does it mean "cease to exist;" but "to be made of none effect" as indeed it is translated in Gal. iii:17 "that it should make the promise of none effect." He hath made Death to be of none effect; or as we should say, to amount to nothing.

But is it really true? Indeed it is; for contrast the cry of the O. T. saint with the joyous word of the N. T. saint as he looks Death squarely in face. The one mourns *"In the cutting off of my days I shall go to the gates of Sheol—I am deprived of the residue of my years. I said I shall not see the Lord, even the Lord, in the land of the living."* The other sings as it were *"We are always confident knowing that whilst present (or at home) in the body we are absent (or away from home) from the Lord (for we walk by faith, not by sight); we are confident, I say, and pleased rather to be away from home from the body and at home with the Lord"* 2 Cor. v:6-7. This is quite a different air, and a much sweeter one; may we learn to sing it more and more clearly.

Let us, dear reader, enjoy another of these happy contrasts together. David groaned: *"O spare me that I may recover strength, before I go hence, and be no more"* Ps. xxxix. But Paul sang: *"For me to live is Christ, and to die is gain . . . but if I live in the flesh, this is the fruit of my labor (i. e. to live is worth my while),yet what I shall choose I* *wot not. For I am in a strait betwixt two, having a desire to depart* and be with Christ which is far better."* To die, gain! To depart, far better. What power has Death over one who can so speak? It does indeed "amount to nothing."

As the soldiers fastened that wretched thief to his cross, he had but a gloomy outlook of an agonizing, lingering death; and then—what? And lo, a word! And darkness again flees, for now he knows that ere the sun sinks to its rest, he shall be with Christ in paradise.† May we not turn back from that scene, and cry across the intervening years to Solomon, "Didst thou not say, a man has no pre-eminence above a beast?" To which of the *beasts* said He at any time, "This day shalt thou be with Me in Paradise"?

"And having stoned Paul, they drew him out of the city, supposing he had been dead." There was

---

*Dr. Bullinger is so intent on proving Death to be an anæsthetic or unconscious sleep, that he insists that the word translated "depart" should be "the return" [of the Lord Jesus] and it is for *this* Paul has the desire. Follow this out, and you have the Apostle saying "nevertheless to abide in the flesh is more needful for you than that the Lord Jesus should return. I am more needful than Christ." Who can have bewitched men that they thus gratuitously strive against their own blessing: "cut *themselves* with stones," as it were? Aye, but who who ever did this, but those under the control of the Devil?

†The labored effort to prove that the Lord is impressing on the thief that he is not speaking to him on any other day than "*this* day," is hardly worthy of serious argument.

the bruised body, quite unconscious, being dragged through the dirt in utter dishonor, but where was the spirit? Well, at all events, it was 14 years after this that he wrote: *"I knew a man in Christ fourteen years ago, whether in the body I cannot tell, or whether out of the body, I cannot tell; God knoweth: such an one caught up to the third heaven— into Paradise."* Why should we doubt or question that during the journey of the bruised body in shame and dishonor through the streets of Lycaonia, the spirit was caught up to the place of departed spirits of the redeemed, and received its highest honor: God's honoring thus answering to the Devil's shame. And of what sweet comfort it is that this was not written of one of such official dignities as an apostle; of such spiritual attainments as Paul; or none of us might share that comfort; but of just a man "in Christ;" so that any—the poorest, feeblest youngest "in Christ" will surely follow in the same path; and, if falling asleep, the body "sown in dishonor," the spirit shall at once be in a glory soon to be shared by the body, too. Oh, art thou in Christ—is He thine all—my reader? What momentous issues hang upon the answer!

Let us note, too, for our further comfort, that this man "in Christ" was so free of all self-occupation in Paradise, that he did not even know whether he was out of the body, or not. But this tells us that Paul knew perfectly well that it is possible to hear and see, and be conscious whilst *out of the body;* for were this not the case, he would have been quite able to tell that, since he *was* conscious, he must have been still in it.

Further note, that he had no difficulty in recognizing *where* he was, for was it not his own home? Surely it was; and may we not say that every one "in Christ" will feel quite at home at once? What a comfort!

Well, my beloved, if for breath to cease, for heart to stop, for pulse to throb no more, is "gain," to be "with Christ" in "Paradise"; in the "third heaven"; "at home with the Lord"; is not Death *"ours";* a servant as every other minister? (1 Cor. iii?) And is he not, as the King of Terrors, abolished?

Ah, yes! even the *certainty* of Death is gone. It is by no means sure that the eye that now reads these lines shall ever "close in death"; for is it not written *"We shall not all sleep"* 1 Cor. xv; and did not even Paul put himself, and encourage the young Thessalonian Christians to put themselves, amongst those who should be *"alive and remain"* to the Lord's coming? (1 Thess. iv.) What a hope! Long deferred indeed it has been; but it will not seem long when—in His company, and changed to be like Himself—we look back on the days now so often dreary.

Sickness, and pain, and weakness are around us still on every side. Oh, beloved, to hear Him say to us in all the wild storm these often make in our

THE CHRISTIAN'S VIEW OF DEATH.

spirits: *"Be not afraid, it is I."* *"My grace is sufficient for thee,"* so shall we triumph still, even through all these.

The new, strange conditions, in which those who are called to depart, may be as they were before His Death and Resurrection. But no—not if it is to be *with Him*—oh, no, that makes an infinite difference.

Whilst for those who remain there is still sorrow, the deep places of the soul are broken up; but when faith resumes her place, the *bitterness* goes, and the sorrow becomes only like the beauty of a storm-cloud spanned by a rainbow.

May the same tender grace that has provided this rich comfort grant us to avail of it to the full, so shall we praise Him in a joyous liberty here; and long to be with Him who has abolished Death, and destroyed him who had its power, that is the Devil.

SATAN.

PART III.
SATAN'S PLACE AND DESTINY

CHAPTER XXI.

IN THE HEAVENLIES.

Contents.

Popular ideas of present dwelling quite false.—Has dwelling on earth with access to the heavens.—How many heavens are there?—The Host of Heaven—Connection between the spiritual and material host of heaven.—Other worlds than ours.—Suggestion of the eternal service of the redeemed in the heavenlies.

We are now ready to consider the remaining portion of our subject: the present place, and future destiny of the Devil; and again following the precedent already established, we will first look at the common, or popular, notion. This is, in this case, exceedingly vague and contradictory. At one moment the Devil is assumed to be in hell; at another, or indeed the same, upon the earth; from heaven alone, however, is he in the popular idea altogether debarred. Further, he is supposed not to be limited in the least by space; but to be practically omnipresent; and able to manifest himself simultaneously, at any spot, in any quarter of the earth.

Hell is, however, assumed to be his Kingdom; yet he is there rather as a king than a prisoner, for he has full powers of personally communicating with the earth at his will.

Our poet Milton has greatly influenced popular views, and he is probably largely responsible for the false idea of Satan's reigning in the infernal regions. He puts the well known lines into his mouth:

> The mind is its own place, and in itself
> Can make a Heaven of Hell; a Hell of Heaven.
> What matter where, if I be still the same,
> And what I should be, all but less than He
> Whom Thunder hath made greater? Here at least
> We shall be free; the Almighty hath not built
> Here for His envy, will not drive us hence;
> Here we may reign secure, and in my choice
> To reign is worth ambition, though in Hell.
> Better to reign in Hell than serve in Heaven.

But if we define Hell as Gehenna, or the Lake of Fire, it is quite sure that according to God's Word, Satan is not only not there now, but that he has never seen Hell, nor will do so for more than a thousand years hence (Rev. xx).

If by Hell we mean the other scriptural word, so translated in our A. V., *Hades,* or the unseen world, the term is so vague and broad as to permit its covering a possible truth; for the Devil is clearly alluded to in Scripture, not only as "Prince of this world," but as "Prince of the powers *of the air*" (Eph. ii); and again, all the host of evil spiritual powers are called *"the world-rulers of this darkness"* (Eph. vi:12) ; terms that carry a rather confused idea to most minds, and yet giving an unmistakable impression of this earth's atmosphere, the air, being the present abode of the fallen hosts of heaven; the "spiritual powers of wickedness or wicked spirits" of Eph. vi:12. Nor does this lack harmony with what we have already concluded, that to the Devil was committed, at some time in the far-off past, this earth and its related "heaven," the air.

For Scripture clearly speaks of three heavens. Our apostle Paul tells us that he was caught up into the *third* heaven, which in the first place necessitates two others; and in the next, we infer that it was the *third* as counting from where the writer was, on earth. The first would then be that nearest the earth, and touching it, the heaven that belongs to the earth, and that shall pass away with it. Since the birds—those expressive figures in nature of the unseen spiritual powers—fly in it, they are called the birds *of the heavens* (Jer. iv). Using the Tabernacle as a divinely given figure of the heavenlies, this would correspond with *the Court,* which touched, as does the air, the outside world. These atmospheric heavens then form the habitation of the Devil and his hosts; he is "Prince of the powers of the air."

The *second* would be the higher *etherial* heavens, where stars and luminaries are, which, as we have seen, are also figures of the spiritual host of heaven. We may call this the *sidereal* heaven, corresponding with the *holy place* of the Tabernacle. In space, it takes us as far as the powers of man, aided by the most powerful instruments he can make can reach. It is the limit of the field, or sphere, of sight—it is the limit of man's powers unaided by divine revelation.

But this assures us that the third heaven is not only beyond all human powers of investigation, but even of thought or expression. To appropriate the idea the apostle gives us in 2 Cor. xii we might term it the "unspeakable" heavens, wherein is Paradise, the temporary abode of the unclothed spirits of the redeemed from amongst men; wherein, too, is "the Father's House," the final and eternal abode of the same blessed ones, and which is the present dwelling of God. This cannot be located at all physically, for beyond the stars is beyond our possibility of grasping. Nor is it at times so far off but that the eye of a Stephen or a Paul could see One there clearly—One quite beyond the vision of others. It is in *infinity,* and we get into a sphere and terms that the finite mind is incapable of compassing; and where it becomes the purest wisdom simply to listen to the Voice of Divine Revelation speaking from, and of that sphere, by figure and picture familiar to us.

But Satan, by his original creation, had apparently free access to every part of the universe; every

heaven was open to him. He had both royal and
priestly privileges; the earth with its heaven was
the sphere of the former; this was his own "house"
as well as kingdom; yet clearly had he free access to the Throne of God, as representing that
kingdom; so the higher heavens were the sphere
of the latter.

The holy convocations in Israel, when the Lord's
people were gathered around Him, seem to have
had their counterparts in the heavenlies, when these
"ministers of His that do His pleasure" were as-
sembled, as *"Sons"* who had been about their Father's business in the various fields of His universe,
to give account of their ministries.

This would *suggest,* at least, other worlds than
ours as affording scope for such angelic ministries
or governments; and this suggestion would be further confirmed by, and would harmonize with, the
plain fact in Scripture that the term "Host of
Heaven" is applied to both those starry worlds we
see on high, as in Deut. iv:19, etc., and to the unseen spiritual angels (1 Kings, xxii:19), as if there
was a close identification between them.

Further, and it is well worthy of consideration,
the stars are not, strange as it may appear, all stars
of *light,* though they seem so to us. Comparatively
recently heavenly bodies have been discovered that
can only be appropriately described as Stars of
darkness, paradoxical as it may sound. It appears
that there is one star, Argol, that gave astronomers

a great deal of perplexity, for they could not account for the phenomenon which it displayed. It would, at regular intervals, gradually decrease from a star, say of the first magnitude, to about the apparent size and brilliancy of one of the fourth; and then, like one of those revolving lights along our coasts, it would regain its former brilliancy. Astronomers could not account for it, until at length, by the intense delicacy of modern photography, they discovered that a dark mass—a mass always dark— passed at regular intervals before the bright one; and partially obscured it; and was, in fact, a dark star. How perfectly, then, if sorrowfully, do those heavens now picture the unseen heavens, since they, too, contain not only spirits, or angels of light, but also spirits or angels of darkness; and how suggestive of unseen verities is this term Host of Heaven—for thus, by the visible creation would God teach us as to things unseen.

A still further harmony with this is in the added fact that both the material hosts of heaven, and their spiritual counterparts—if the term may be so used—are spoken of as the objects of the distorted worship of mankind (Comp. Deut. iv:19 xxxii: 17).

Thus analogy, at least, clearly suggests that the sidereal worlds are, as our earth, under the government of the spiritual principalities of heaven. And this analogy is strengthened by the clearly revealed fact that, in the smaller sphere of this earth itself, angelic or spiritual princes are identified with its various empires; and that not only are these powers interested spectators of the events of earth, but themselves champion the causes of its empires, Persia, Grecia, etc., and contend for or against the purposes of God as to the earth, seeking to further or to hinder those purposes, which ever tend to bringing Israel in her Messiah to the place of headship among the nations (Dan. x).

May we go one step further and discern a suggestion of the future ministry of the heavenly redeemed in the words *"that in the ages to come* (note the indefiniteness of duration, implying eternity) *he might show the exceeding riches of his grace, in his kindness toward us through Christ Jesus"* (Eph. ii:7). To whom is this to be shown if not to those same principalities and powers to whom even now *"might be known by the church the manifold wisdom of God"* (Eph. iii:10).

I would not strain the words, nor distort them from their evident, simple, and precious prime meaning that the very presence of such outcasts as we—such low and lost sinners—in the highest glory, one with the Son of God the Lord of glory—shall itself show "his grace"—"the riches of his grace"—"the exceeding riches of his grace." But the question is, does this *exhaust* the force of the words? Is it not a perfectly legitimate deduction that this shall form a part at least of that future service of which Rev. xxii speaks: *"And his serv-*

ants shall serve Him" even in taking and telling out to all the universe of worlds, the wondrous display of grace to the sinful and sinning inhabitants of earth. It would be a very blessed ministry for an eternity of time to make known through those innumerable (apparently infinitely so, the infinite and eternal God alone con count them Ps. cxlvii:4), and mighty worlds how great things God hath done for us poor children of earth; and awaken fresh songs from ever widening circles of bliss.

There is another clear thread of analogy to strengthen all this. Israel on the earth has ever afforded figures and types of the unseen. What is part of the service of that genuinely holy and eternally redeemed Israel? It is to spread the tidings of their deliverance to the outlying peoples of the earth, to its remotest bound, throughout that millennial day which prepares the way for, and figures in a sense, Eternity. *"And I will send those that escape of them unto the nations, to Tarshish, Pul and Lud, that draw the bow, to Tubal and Javan, to the isles afar off, that have not heard my fame, neither have seen my glory; and they shall declare my glory among the Gentiles"* (Is. lxvi:19). Hear them: *"O sing unto the Lord a new song; sing unto the Lord all the earth." "Say among the heathen that the Lord reigneth"* (Ps. xcvi). *"God shall bless* us, *and all the ends of the earth shall fear Him,"* is the prophecy in Ps. lxvii:7. *"He hath remembered his mercy and his truth toward the house of Israel; all the ends of the earth have seen the salvation of our God,"* is the fulfilment in Ps. xcviii:3. Put these, and many other Scriptures, together, and it is quite clear that God's salvation of Israel is the basis of making Him known by Israel's missionaries to the ends of the earth, and making all the earth to be one choir of praise.

What Israel does on earth, the heavenly redeemed do in the heavenlies, and they make known His Name and glory to remotest bounds of the universe, and the news they carry awaken melody, till the whole universe becomes a choir of praise to Him that sitteth on the Throne, and the Lamb forever and ever. Surely this is very strongly confirmatory, and would it not be a worthy and joyous ministry? Indeed it would!

CHAPTER XXII.

IN THE HEAVENLIES—CONTINUED.

Contents.

If Satan in heaven, how understand his fall thence (Is. xiv; Luke x:18; John xii:31)?—Why did not God cast him out long ago?—The mystery of God.

But if Satan be still in the heavenlies, in what light are we to consider the passages that speak of his fall or expulsion thence? For instance: *"How art thou fallen from heaven, O Lucifer, son of the morning?"* and again, *"I beheld Satan, as lightning, fall from heaven"* (Luke x:18); and again, *"Now is the judgment of this world;* now *shall the prince of this world be cast out"* (John xii:31). All these would appear to teach us that Satan was cast out of heaven in some far distant past age; and, even, from this world, at the hour of the Lord's death; for clearly this is the "hour" in view in John xii:27.

That he has not yet been literally cast out of this world is but too sadly evident; and we are compelled to interpret this Scripture, at least, in the light of others that fully recognize what is, as a matter of fact, so incontestable. In Job's first chapter he is seen, in that past day, as having unbarred access to the presence of Jehovah amid the Sons of God. In Ephesians vi he is seen, in this present day, still in the heavenlies, as prince of these "spiritual powers of wickedness" that resist the heavenly redeemed from enjoying their inheritance; and even a sure look into the future shows him to us in Rev. xii still in heaven—even then not yet cast out, and it recognizes that he has ever been there through all the time intervening.

Then surely the Scriptures that speak of this as an accomplished fact, must not, and cannot possibly be, interpreted in the strictly literal sense in which we are accustomed to use them; but the "fall from heaven" of Isaiah may have a strictly *moral* significance—and speak of a total loss of a place of highest privilege in the complacent favor of his Creator. Just as our Lord said, *"And thou, Capernaum, which art exalted to heaven, shall be brought down to hell* (hades)," most clearly refers to the surpassing privileges enjoyed by that city, and not a literal exaltation, nor casting down, at all from a literal Heaven to a literal Hell. In such passages Heaven speaks of highest privilege; Hell of deepest abasement and loss of all such.

So with our Lord's words in Luke: they do not necessarily mean that He, in some more or less remote past, had seen some literal and final expulsion of Satan from heaven—the fact that other Scriptures clearly show him there still, positively forbids such a thought. But it would appear very simple if the words of the returned Seventy, *"Lord, even the demons are subject unto us through Thy name"* (v:17), called up before the eye of the Lord Jesus, in a backward glance, the loss of all his privileges when iniquity was found in him, and in a forward one, the final downfall of the enemy of man. Here, in this subjection of the evil spirits, he sees the earnest of that literal fall out of the heavens, that actually and literally takes place long afterwards, yet so sure is it, as to be spoken of as a past fact;* and indeed in this sense may have been said to have taken place from the very beginning.

In the same way John xii. The Greeks, or Gentile proselytes from dark heathendom as they were, were still unsatisfied; their hearts hungered still; they *"would see Jesus."* They had found truth in Judaism; but it was far more bitter than sweet; and thus it made them hungry for more, as men take "bitters" only to awaken appetite. All is deeply symbolic. Gentiles are coming to the Light of Israel (Is. lx), for here He is purely *divine;* and as such, He is the God, "not of the Jews only, but of the Gentiles also."

The Lord Jesus recognizes the deep significance of the moment; and speaks as "Son of Man,"

---

*Compare Rom. viii:30 "whom he justified, then he also *glorified."* So sure it is, that whilst still future, it is spoke of as actually past.

through whom alone all the nations of the earth are to be blessed. But for that blessing, the *"Corn of wheat must fall into the ground and die."* Thus, at this moment, His Cross and sufferings come before Him; it is the Gethsemane of John's gospel but without the agony and bloody sweat, which would be inconsistent with His divine dignity here. He speaks, however, in full view of that Cross when He says, *"Now is the judgment of this world, now shall the prince of this world be cast out."*

In one aspect, His death is the passing away of judgment from the penitent self-judged believer; in another, it is the *basis* of judgment, not actually present, but yet to come, on an unbelieving world, which is fully manifested in all its awful state in His shameful death at its hands.

So with regard to the casting out of Satan from the earth—He is *not* cast out of the world yet, but reigns still as a usurper; nay, it is Messiah Himself who is "cut off and has nothing" in accord with Daniel's prophecy (Ch. ix :26). It is the Son and Heir—Son of Man—who is cast out of the vineyard; but the *basis* on which Satan will be actually cast out is laid in that death; it removes every obstacle, and nothing but the execution remains. God could not, as it were, inflict judgment on the world till provision was made for His own dear people. He could not pass through Egypt till the Lamb was slain, and His people sheltered by its blood. But as soon as the paschal lamb *is* slain, Egypt lay open to judgment; and even as that lamb dies, might it not have been said, "now is the judgment of Egypt"? That was but a picture of the larger sphere we have in John xii, with the addition of the effect of that cross on Satan's abiding here. He, Satan, would cast out the true prince, the Son; and Heir of the vineyard, and kill Him; but in the doing this he himself unconsciously lays the basis for himself to be cast out.

But it is at least not an unnatural question: Why could not God cast out the enemy at any time? Why must his expulsion await the death of God's beloved Son? Why let all these long weary ages of sin, sorrow, tears, and blood, intervene? "Why not God kill debbil?" as the African heathen constantly ask their missionaries, is quite a *natural* question. Or at least why not restrain him from further evil and mischief?

If *power* were all that God desired to display, this might possibly have been at the very first; but if He would by means of the very eruption of evil make known the infinite depths of His love and wisdom, making the eater yield meat, the strong sweetness, by bringing a captive race into liberty and blessing, then can we at least conceive, in some degree, a worthy motive for the delay. And for the rest, we may await, in patience, the sounding of that seventh trumpet, when *"the mystery of God"* in permitting, not merely the introduction, not merely the continuance, but the *apparent* triumph of evil—*"shall be finished,"* and, in that day of full display, He shall be justified of all, as now He is of His children.

But even now we can see that if the race of men has become so linked with Satan by a common nature with him, as to necessitate *his* expulsion, involving equally that of the race, then the display of that power, if there is to be salvation for men at all, must await what infinite wisdom, combined with infinite love, alone can do, to meet the case and deliver mankind. In that Cross of the Lord Jesus—the sins of all who believe were judged. Sin itself was condemned, and the basis is laid for the casting out of Satan, with those only who still voluntarily cleave to him.

Thus the words in no case involve a literal, actual, present loss of his place either in heaven or the earth; but again and again they sound the knell of his fate, in the certainty of that loss.

His *"place"* then is now *in the heavens,* and will be until a certain event which we will now consider.

CHAPTER XXIII.

THE WAR IN HEAVEN.

Contents.

Can one wonder at the attacks of the enemy on the doctrine of *Atonement by Blood?* He will leave us all the religion, all the so-called Christianity that we want, if he can but eliminate from it all that can be an answer to his accusations, put him to silence, bring to nothing all his hopes of finding a spot of unrighteousness on the Throne of God; and lead to the loss of all place in heaven and earth forever. To-day the *popular* teaching does eliminate this altogether; and far less to be feared is any amount of open infidelity, than this Satanic attack which is masked behind Christian profession, and high-sounding religious titles. These teachers, in conformity with their master, appear as "ministers of righteousness," and make their attack on this foundation of our faith under that plea. "Is it righteous," they indignantly cry, "for a just one to be punished for the guilty? Would it be just to hang an innocent man in the place of the real murderer?"

"No, indeed," we answer, "if the innocent be *compelled* to endure the penalty of the guilty, that would be gross injustice; but if there be perfect voluntariness on the part of all the parties to the transaction, first of the government or law, next of the substitute, and finally of the criminal—no forcing of any—then is it absolutely righteous, and the expression of a love as sublime as the degree of suffering involved. The *principle* is of diurnal occurrence in human courts without challenge. A poor man, guilty of some offense, is fined. A friend, quite voluntarily, pays the fine, or gives him the money wherewith to do it. If he is *willing* to offer, and the debtor to accept, such kindness, no one thinks of protesting, or accusing of unrighteousness.

This is indeed a minor matter, but the *principle* is the same; it is only a question of degree. *Voluntary* substitution is in perfect accord with absolute justice; provided that every step *is* voluntary; the substitute in offering, the government in permitting, the criminal in accepting.

Well, when that is done which not even Michael himself, with all the holy powers of Heaven, could effect, and not even Satan, with all his angels, could prevent, is it to be wondered that the time has come for the place of these evil ones to be found in Heaven, no more forever. Heaven cannot contain both justified sinners and Him that has forever accused them. If God is just in justifying them, then Satan is unjust in accusing; and an unjust accusation renders the accuser as guilty as the accused would have been, were it just. Heaven can have no place for such; he must be cast out. If a place has been "prepared" for the one the other has lost his place forever.

There is another scene in the heavens, that must be closely connected with the Devil's final expulsion thence, and must therefore be looked at now.

In 2 Cor., ch. v, we read: *"We must all be manifested before the judgment seat of Christ."* This is clearly a statement of a most solemn fact which is of universal application. There is no escape for any, either saint or sinner, from that Judgment Seat; and this is further strengthened by that corresponding word in Rom xiv:12: *"So then every one of us shall give an account of himself to God."* Neither Scripture, you will note, specifies where, or when that Judgment Seat is set up; nor whether it be once or often; it is a broad general statement.

But does not this clash with, and destroy that most precious feature of the gospel the Lord Himself announced: *"Verily, verily, I say unto you, he that heareth my word, and believeth on him that sent me, hath everlasting life, and* SHALL

NOT COME INTO JUDGMENT, *but is passed from death unto life*" (John v:24). How can the believer both "be manifested before the Judgment Seat," and yet "not come into judgment"?

We are quite sure both are absolutely true—we, believers, cannot possibly come into that awful judgment whose dread penalty our Saviour has borne on the Cross; and yet there is a real need for us to be *manifested* before the Judgment Seat of Christ; not to be tried as prisoners to see what is to be our eternal lot; but one can see at least three other and worthy reasons: First, in order that that solemnizing truth may have its effect on our lives here; on every step of our journey; on every crisis. Were this at all realized, would it not solve many a perplexity and do away with frivolity and lightness. None can overestimate its value in guiding right in times of trial; let the event be seen in the light of that Judgment Seat, and it will at once lead to a right course.

Next, there is just one thing necessary before entering eternity. We are like Jacob in Gen. xxxv going up "to Bethel (i. e., God's House) to dwell there" and forever. Must not everything be suited to the place, the *Father's House* our Bethel, to which we go? We need—we *must have,* as did Jacob at that time, *everything clearly and fully out;* so fully, so clearly, that it will not do to trust our own memory to bring it out. We need the Lord "who loved us and gave Himself for us," to do that

THE WAR IN HEAVEN.

He will. And if the thought is solemn, is it not blessed too? Is it not a happy thing that, ere eternity begins, full provision is made for the perfect security of its peace—for a communion that may not be marred by a thought of anything overlooked or forgotten.

In the third place, and as another reason for this Judgment Seat, it is *in order that each may receive the things [done] in the body according to what he did, whether good or evil.* That Judgment Seat clearly manifests, not merely the external appearance, but the very essence of motive of all the deeds done in the body of every one who appears before it, and these tell the story of what each has been. In each saint's life there will be a long dark line of dead works—they manifest his condition at that time. Then a change, and, the works whilst still imperfect, and needing to be washed in the blood of the Lamb (Rev. vii:17) radiate with a new life, a new motive, a new power. Yet, even now, ever and anon, there is a black mark speaking even of the believer having "sown to the flesh."

All this is burnt, as wood, hay, stubble, as 1 Cor. iii:15 teaches—wherever or whenever it may have occurred before or after regeneration*—all is burnt up; and only that which is of God remains.

*The objection raised to this by some, that all our sins prior to our conversion, having been blotted out by, and through the blood of Christ, and God's saying that He will remember them no more, it is impossible for them ever to come up again, rests upon a very defective

SATAN.

It is a test of works, but works as manifesting the person; and now are the rewards of every believer according to the fidelity of each.

It remains for us to ask *where* is the Judgment Seat of Christ set up before which believers must be manifested? It is surely not on the earth, prior to their rapture to the air : all Scripture clearly negatives this. It is equally surely not after they "are manifested with Him in glory;" for then they come not to be judged; but, with Him, to judge the world (1 Cor. vi). It must be then at some time between that rapture and that revelation.

The Judgment Seat, before which believers must appear, must then necessarily be in the heavenlies. Blessed Comfort! They are in heaven even when they are manifested before the Judgment Seat, there can be no question of their *going* there. Aye, and would we have further comfort? Then look at the

view of that work, and of the Gospel; little as this is suspected by the objectors. They quite confuse Judgment of the Person for salvation, and the person being manifest by works, before the Judgment Seat. *Penally, all* sins not only before but after conversion too are equally gone forever. If but one sin, let it be after God's grace has brought us to Himself—*one* sin only be thus remembered—not "blotted out"—what would be the awful result? Surely that precious blood answers for *all* sin, whenever committed, whilst *every deed "in the body,"* with no limit as to time, the Scripture says, there manifests the person; and whilst this is solemn, it is blessed; whilst blessed, it is certainly solemn : oh what songs it will awaken, that such creatures as we are there and forever!

THE WAR IN HEAVEN.

Judge, be not afraid; regard Him patiently and well; He bears many a mark whereby you may know Him. See His Hands and His Feet; and behold, His Side! The judicial penalty for all the evil that is manifest has been borne by Him. What songs, again I say, it will awaken!

So that, apparently, during the same interval, between the Rapture and the Revelation these two events "The Judgment Seat of Christ" and "The War in Heaven" must take place. May we reverently inquire as to the *order* of these two; which comes first?

We must at once confess to not having any direct Scripture, and therefore we must not speak dogmatically, yet perhaps our God may, in His grace, have given us such revelation of His ways with men that we may feel that we have some solid basis for an answer to this question from analogy.

Is it in accord with those ways for God to deal with *His children* in the presence of their accusers? That He *justifies* these with the utmost publicity is most blessedly clear. When He says I have "not beheld iniquity in Jacob," nor "perverseness in Israel" it is full in the face of Balak, even challenging him to pay the closest attention: *Rise up Balak and hear; hearken unto me thou son of Zippor,"* but when He deals with His people Himself, He never exposes them before a hostile gaze—*that* is a private matter between Him and them. See how He protects the name of His dear servant, John the

Baptist, even when sending to him a word of gracious warning with the repeated "What went ye out for to see?"

We may recall that in that first recorded scene of judgment we have in Scripture not one word of the sentence is pronounced on our first parents, guilty though they were, till the curse had been pronounced on their tempter and would-be accuser.

Thus here, without, again be it said, venturing to speak dogmatically, yet we gather that the sentence shall surely be again passed on the Devil in heaven, and he cast out *prior to the manifestation of the heavenly saints before the Judgment Seat of Christ.*

The war in heaven terminates and the consequent casting out thence of Satan takes place, in the midst of the last week of Daniel's great prophecy, for $3\frac{1}{2}$ years after this, the Lord comes to execute judgment (Rev. xii). Thus we conclude that it is fitting that it should be in the quiet of a cleansed Heaven that the Bride should make herself ready (Rev. xix) and the Lord be able to present her to Himself "a glorious church, not having spot, nor wrinkle, nor any such thing."

But has there been any clear evidence of the everlasting acceptance of the Lord's people? Indeed there has; for as the *resurrection* of the Lord Jesus was full proof of the divine acceptance of both Himself and His work, so the resurrection of His people is full proof of *their* acceptance and

justification. In it, the glory of God shines out
with a radiancy far beyond, but of the same kind,
as on the day in which Lazarus heard His voice,
and came forth of his grave. It would seem as if
that warrior, Michael the Archangel, mustering the
hosts of those redeemed from the grave, recognizes
that this is such a revelation of the glory of God,
as to leave the Accuser, still posing as ever as The
Cherub that Covereth, and as having the Righteousness of God in view, not one foot of standing
ground in the heavenlies; and, prior to all judgment, the war in heaven begins with the result of
the expulsion of Satan.

How deeply significant are the Leaders' names
in this war. On the one side is he who from the
beginning would *be as God;* and, by leading mankind along the same path as himself, he has brought
them into the dust of death. *Now* at the moment
that the glory of God is displayed in the resurrection of redeemed men from that dust; saving
them out of death; what wonder if one springs
forward, in indignant protest against any such
claimant, whose own name, *Michael,* shall be his
battle cry *"Who is as God?"* *"Thou* claim to be as
God! *Thou,* who can only accuse the guilty; whilst
God, our God, has found a way of even justly
justifying them! *Thou* as *God!* Oh, in view of
these glorified hosts, not one of whom has not
known what *sin*—thy work—is, yet, here, and

without a spot, I cry out again as a battle cry my name, *"Michael!"* *"Who* is as God?"

The war is over; and Satan is cast out; but lest there should be the slightest question that the names by which he has been known belong to different personalities; all four are given here. The Devil, as the Liar; Satan, as the Murderer in the heavenlies; The Old Serpent, as the Liar; and The Dragon, as the Murderer on the earth.

In the calm that follows the conflict each saint, with no accuser present to condemn, is still manifested; as one poor woman was long before (Jno. viii) but in *their* case, everyone has, in varying measure, *praise* of God" (1 Cor. iv) and each one "sins no more" forever.

CHAPTER XXIV.

Satan Confined to the Earth.

Contents.

When the Devil has been thus cast out of Heaven, his energies, if not his aims, must have a more limited sphere; but they are still of exactly the same character, as seeking to maintain his unrivalled sway over the earth, and mankind upon it: he would still "be as God"—the god of this world still. So that then he takes complete control of its politics, undisguised, and in his own true character. Not, as now, with the pretension of being still an "angel of light," and often permitting the government, whether supreme or subsidiary, being in the hand of upright and even pious rulers, as we have had many examples in all countries; a fact too that is in itself suggestive of One higher than Satan, Who still maintains supreme control, and thus answers His people's prayers and intercessions for Kings and all in authority (1 Tim. ii).

But in order to get a clear view of the sequence of events as Scripture alone throws its sure light into the future, we must take a glance—it can be but that—at the happenings on the earth whilst the war, of which we have been speaking, is going on in the heavens.

The Lord Jesus has left His Seat at the right hand of the Majesty on High, has come to the earth—heavens or air; and by the Trump of God, by the mighty attraction of His Person, by the sound of His Voice in a gathering shout, has drawn up to Himself all who have acknowledged that attraction, and heard that Voice, in any measure, in their life-time (1 Thess. iv).

This leaves the earth without the presence of the Church, and without the Spirit of God, as an abiding Presence. Evil is therefore unhindered in its development—"He who lets, or hinders," being thus "gone out of the way" (2 Thess. ii:7).

At first we have grounds for assuming the contrast is not so striking; and this may well be accounted for by the Devil and his angels being occupied in that "war in heaven" at which we have looked. Thus occupied, and being neither omnipresent, nor omniscient, nor omnipotent, the affairs of earth cannot receive that personal attention that would develop in an absolute rejection of all divine claims instantly.

Things are therefore rather negatively than positively evil. One might perhaps naturally expect that they would be, if anything, morally better than they are now, for the Devil is otherwise engaged, and the mysterious rapture of so many (1 Thess. iv) may well have a sobering effect for a time.

In this favorable condition of things, Zionism, as it is called, comes to full fruition: that is, the national existence of the Jews as a separate State, is recovered. Some strong maritime power, *that sendeth ambassadors by the sea, even in vessels of**

---

*Is. xviii. This short but most interesting chapter is worthy of much prayerful meditation but it is not in direct connection with our subject. However, the word "bulrushes" in v2 is a translation of a Hebrew word, *gohmeh,* coming from a root *gahmah, "to drink up,"* and thus bears in it the idea of *water-consuming.* Now the papyrus, or bulrush, does this, but "vessels of *bulrushes*" would be neither very safe, nor swift; nor do we know ot anything of the kind to-day. But the modern *steamship* could hardly be better described in prophetic language than as a "WATER-CONSUMING VESSEL," especially as the word rendered "vessel" has in it the idea of *intricate construction,* with a definite purpose; whilst finally, the address, *"Go, ye swift messengers,"* seems to make one assured that the Holy Spirit is thus describing, in the only possible way the language of that far-off time permitted, the *steamship* of *the last days.* Some of us have assumed that this chapter described, or foretold, the actual return of the scattered Jews to Palestine by means of the swift steamships of the power addressed. But this must not be too hastily adopted. The language appears to me, now, rather *bulrushes upon the waters* [saying], *Go, ye swift messengers to a nation scattered and peeled, to a people terrible from their beginning hitherto."* Is. xviii:2, thus takes them under its shadowing or protecting wing. By this alliance the returned nation puts itself under the protection of the United States of Europe under *their* federal head, "the prince." Dan. ix:27 thus reads: *"And he* (the prince of the Roman Empire, then revived in a ten-kingdom form with one Supreme Emperor) *"shall confirm a covenant with the mass"* (of the Jewish

---

to favor their being there already. And the swift steamships bearing ambassadors to them. Why should this not be in order to make that covenant for seven years referred to in Dan. ix:27? Nor do the words *"land shadowing with wings beyond the rivers of Cush"* appear to me, now, to designate so clearly some particular *nation,* like Great Britain, as I had once thought, but it would seem to be quite capable of application to a *"land"* rather than a *nation*: a land beyond the two rivers of Cush—that is, both the Asiatic and African Cush; and, therefore, may mean all Europe—confederated Europe. The question is not without practical importance in the interpretation of the prophetic Scriptures; for, apart from this, is there any Old Testament Scripture that *directly* foretells or describes the *actual* return, or transportation, of the Jews *in unbelief?* If not, it leaves it open to occur *prior* to the rapture of the heavenly redeemed without contravening the principle accepted by many that, until that rapture, God will not definitely recommence His work with His earthly people, and Old Testament prophecy will, therefore, await fulfilment. In other words we *may* still be on earth when this return occurs, although of course not necessarily so.

people, or Daniel's people, who are the direct subjects of the prophecy), *for one week* (of years, or seven years). And this covenant remains in full force for half the period of its "life," or three and a half years. Then some strange thing happens that alters everything. To this we will recur directly; but as we have thus briefly traced the course of events with the Jews, we must equally briefly run over the divinely foretold history of the prophetic Gentile world during the same period.

Men do not need the express intervention of the Devil to war with one another; and the catching up of the Church;* whilst, as has been said, it may have some effect, yet will not result in peace on earth, nor prevent those providential interpositions of God in judgment as foretold in the earlier seals of Rev. vi. Wars of an intensely sanguinary character, followed by famine and pestilence (Rev. vi: 1-8) soak Europe in blood; till out of the conflict arises one, hitherto little esteemed—a "little horn," Dan. vii—who, by his surpassing military genius, conquers three opposing powers (Dan. vii:8), and succeeds where both Charlemagne and the First Napoleon failed, in *re*-forming, after a long period of non-existence, the Roman Empire ("which was, and is not, and shall be present" (Rev. xvii:8), only now it is composed of ten kingdoms which unite in

---

*I specify the Church as being the living ones on earth at that time, but not at all as doubting that the rapture includes all the heavenly saints of both dispensations.

giving their fealty to this conqueror, who thus becomes the Prince of the Roman world (Dan. vii:2; ix:27; Rev. xiii; xvii:12, etc.), and in whom we find the individual who makes a covenant with "the many" of the Jews in their land—already referred to.

Those two prominent actors in the crucifixion of Christ, the Jew and the Roman Empire, after a prolonged period of national death and burial, must be raised again (Is. xxvi; Rev. xvii), that God may again take up the thread of this world's history where it was dropped, when His heavenly purposes as to the Church began.

How many years it will take to get things into this position I am not aware that Scripture tells us—it must take more than a few, probably *many;* but this is of no practical importance. And whether the Rapture of the heavenly saints will take place before any of these events take place, or only just prior to the forming of the treaty or covenant for seven years, I am not aware that we are told.

We must, however, pursue our inquiry a little further, and equally rapidly.

By conquest, and by treaty, peace has at length become established in Europe. But this only clears the way for another, and an *internal* convulsion, which racks the body politic. Rumblings of discord are audible enough even to-day, in the growing Socialism in its various forms—a general widespread feeling of discontent, fostered and increased by the increasing concentration of wealth, and by constantly more wide-spread education, leading all to consider themselves adapted for a higher station, and greater wealth than is their lot. Finally, in a time of financial distress and want amongst the lower classes, (Rev. viii :7) a terrific revolution, only to be likened to an earthquake, breaks out, by which all the authorities and rulers, from the Supreme head (sun) to the petty magistrates (stars) are over-thrown; for so we read the clearly figurative language of Rev. viii :12.

This then is the situation in the midst of that last week of years—the Jews are then in their land, without any manifestation of any pious remnant amongst them, for all together are worshipping Jehovah in the one Temple and morning and evening sacrifices are smoking once again on the altar of Burnt Offering. Amongst the Gentiles is discontent, finally resulting in a revolution, so thorough and widespread as to subvert all authority, and the dream of the modern anarchist, or nihilist, seems fully realized.

At just this juncture on earth, the war in heaven comes to its end; and Satan and his hosts are cast down to the earth. He knows that he has but a short time (Rev. xii) ; his long day is fast drawing to its close; how shall he make the most of its remaining moments? How can he better employ them than by stamping out of earth—*his* earth—all recognition of the God whom he has dared and still dares to rival? And he will add infinite venom to that rivalry by again imitating that supreme act of Divine grace, in taking man into partnership with himself, and making that puny creature a sharer in, or the expressor of, his own rivalry with God.

His first act then is to restore the Gentile government that has been overthrown. He lifts up the fallen monarch of the Roman Empire, re-seats him upon his throne, and now, he, whom everyone thought to have been definitively and irrevocably destroyed—or, in the language of Scripture— *"wounded to death,"* is once more re-established, but now, he owes his "power, and throne, and great authority" directly to the Dragon (Rev. xiii:3-4).

Well may the Scripture speak of this empire as coming "up from the abyss" (Rev. xvii:8), the destined prison of its founder (Rev.xx:2-3). For Satan himself now fully energizes its head, controls him absolutely; and he breaks the covenant he had made with the returned Jews (Is. xxxiii:8) ; puts a sudden and peremptory stop to their worship of Jehovah; "causes the sacrifice and oblation to cease" (Dan. ix:27) ; and, having great wrath, seeks to annihilate all who persist in the recognition of God (Rev. xii: 12-13).

Let us next inquire what is the effect of all this upon the Jews returned to their land? As to the mass, the broken covenant affects them little: they with Antichrist (1 John ii:18) or the False Prophet (Rev. xix:20), who is still a *king* (Dan. xi:36), and "the man of sin, the son of perdition" (2 Thess. ii:3), remain in closest alliance with this diabolically re-instated Roman Emperor; and indeed make another covenant which is now directly with those exponents of evil, "Death and Hades" (Is. xxviii:15).*

It is this, and at this time, that the Devil caps the climax of all his imitations, by forming a perfect one of the Divine Trinity on the earth, with the supreme authority, or God the Father, represented by the Gentile; God the Son by the Jewish Antichrist or False Prophet; and he himself, energizing all, taking the place of the Holy Spirit.

The centre of all his activity is in Jerusalem; for here alone is there a complete testimony to "the God of the earth" in the symbolic "two witnesses" of Rev. xi, who thus represent a portion at least of a God-fearing remnant, now fully manifested in the lurid glare of the fiercest persecution. These are called Zion's travail-pains: and *"as soon as Zion travailed, she brought forth her children* (Is. lxvi:8) ; that is, if I understand the Scripture rightly, this pious and true remnant hitherto undistinguished from the mass, are now, by persecution, *evidenced,* and *at once,* as the nucleus of the new nation. But vast numbers of these suffer martyrdom rather than

---

*The covenant spoken of in Dan. ix:27 must be carefully distinguished from that of Is. xxviii. The former was effected at the beginning; the latter in the middle of the last week of seven years. The former was rather benevolent in character: the latter utterly and diabolically malevolent towards everything divine.

conform to the diabolical idolatry of the day, and
for still maintaining Jehovah to be the true God of
all the earth (Rev. xi:4).

For the "Abomination of Desolation," or the Idol
Image that results in desolation (Rev. xiii:14; Matt.
xxiv:15) is now set up in the Holy Place; and that
nation that has been so *"many days without a King,
and without a prince, and without a sacrifice, and
without an image, and without an ephod, and without teraphim"* (Hos. iii), since the return from
Babylon; but whose house thus "empty, swept, and
garnished" is now filled with seven demons far
worse than the first, voluntarily worships the Image
of the Beast, at the command of their False Messiah, the False Prophet (Rev. xiii).

Throughout what is known as Christendom, there
is at this time but one church, one religion; a com-
bination of apostate Roman Catholicism, apostate
Protestantism, apostate Judaism,* all pervaded and

---

*Since the above was written, the following extracts
are taken from an article in The Literary Digest of 22
January, 1910, entitled, JEWISH ATTITUDE TOWARD JESUS."
Dr. Isidor Singer, "an eminent Jewish scholar" says, "A
new theology is knocking at the pulpit of priest, pastor,
and rabbi. Everyone of them feels the old theological
platform giving way under his feet. The hour seems to
be at hand when Roman Catholic, Protestant, and Jew,
and whoever believes in one personal God, and the moral
order of the universe (sic), shall be able and willing to
gather about the same monotheistic banner." And the
well-known New York banker, Mr. Jacob H. Schiff, says,
"We Jews honor and revere Jesus of Nazareth as we do

held together by the "slime" of modern Commercialism: the history of Dan. iii repeating itself marvellously in another Babylon (Rev. xvii.).

Every pulpit sends forth a stream of doctrinal poison like smoke from the pit, that hides all true light, and vitiates that sustainer of life: the air (Rev. ix). God and His Christ are everywhere blasphemed; man is everywhere exalted (has it not even now begun? Indeed did it not begin in the day of 2 Thess. ii:7?) and Satan has everything his own way.

So passes away the last three and a half years of this age; and at the end of that time it would appear that the God-fearing Jewish remnant (history again repeating itself) "doing exploits," as their types, the Maccabean heroes of the past (Dan. xi:32), take, as their last exploit, forcible possession of their city. The news of this reaches, and much disturbs, the false King, who is in Egypt on a career of conquest (Dan. xi:44). He returns, and, calling his allies to his aid, the combined forces, consisting of all the nations of the prophetic, or Roman earth, lay siege

---

our own prophets that preceded him." That is, a common platform for these three contending divisions in the sphere of Christendom is on the point of being found in the acceptance of Jesus as a prophet, in the rejection of Jesus as God manifest in the flesh: The Son of God, one with the Father.

This may well pave the way for the first covenant of Dan. ix:27; that of Is. xxviii:15 will be the outcome of far more violent rejection of *everything* of God, and of the Lord Jesus Christ in every way.

to Jerusalem, capture it (Zech. xiv), but even as the news of its fall flashes through the earth, and men, with a sigh of relief, say "Peace—Safety at last, for those troublesome Jews are annihilated" (1 Thess. v); and it looks as if the last spark of divine life amongst men would be quenched, and as if, therefore, "no flesh would be saved" (Matt. xxiv:22), the days *are* shortened;* the Lord Jesus

---

It is thus I understand the Lord's words in Matt. xxiv—: *"Except those days should be shortened, there should no flesh be saved,"* which may be interpreted in the light of Is. lxv:8 *"As the new wine is found in the cluster, and one saith Destroy it not for a blessing is in it: so I will do for* MY SERVANTS' SAKE *that I may not destroy them all.* From this one gathers that the *"flesh"* of Matt. xxiv is the race of mankind: the pious remnant of Israel is *"the cluster."* The hope of the whole race lies in that "cluster"; and if that cluster be destroyed, or that remnant be really wiped out, then no flesh would be saved; the link connecting mankind with God—the only thing that He owns on earth—would be snapped and nothing would remain possible but that all should be swept away in judgment. It is at the moment when this appears inevitable, that the days are suddenly cut off short (for this is the idea in the word Koloboo: "docked like the tail of a horse") by the appearing of the Deliverer: Jesus.

The word "saved" in Matt. xxiv is in view of earth's government in harmony with the whole character of that gospel. Are men to be completely identified with Satan, and so lost, or with God and so saved? Of course this involves eternal issues.

The shortening of the days does not mean that God's purposes are in any way changed for their number is told with absolute precision: 1260; Dan. xii, Rev. xii; but when

is revealed from heaven with His mighty angels in flaming fire (2 Thess. ii).

And now the Devil's place on earth is lost to him, and he is cast, bound, into the Abyss, his prison for one thousand years. But this we will consider in the next chapter.

———

everything is going exactly as Satan would have it, the days are suddenly cut off short.

CHAPTER XXV.

IN THE ABYSS.

Contents.

The result of His Coming.—The end of Lucifer's government of earth.—The 1,000 years of Christ's reign.—Is the Abyss literally in the centre of the earth?—The moral force of scriptural terms "height" and "depth"—"up" and "down."

Thus the Lord Jesus Christ now comes to judge the earth; that earth that has been the scene of so many conflicts between the forces of good and evil; that earth that was originally under Lucifer's government, and has all through the ages been still claimed by him as the Devil; that earth given to man, whose title is now made good and good forever in the Second Man, who comes to *"cast out of His Kingdom all things that offend"* and to reign over it to its utmost bounds.

But first His Judgment Seat is again set up; not in the heaven this time, but on the earth. We may read of it both in Dan. vii and Matt. xxv. Before Him are gathered all the nations—there are no "nations" in the spiritual world—they distinguish the *earth*; but this judgment—which can hardly be instantaneous, but gradual—is again pre-

ceded by a further humiliation of our subject.
Satan is becoming weaker now. A single angel
now binds him, who was above all angels, with a
chain, and he is cast out of the earth, every name
by which he has been known in his dealings with
men being, as when cast out of heaven, again given
him: The Dragon, Old Serpent, Devil and Satan,
so that there may again be no question as to his
identity, or any thought that one of these may remain. For a thousand years he is shut up as a
prisoner in the Abyss (Rev. xx. 1-3). Note how the
prophecy of Isaiah (Ch. xxiv. 21-23) and that of
Revelation mutually supplement one another. The
O. T. prophet sees Jehovah intervening at length in
the earth, which He has apparently left so long to
the enemy and lo it is "utterly broken," "clean dis-
solved," "moved exceedingly," staggers like a
drunken man," "shakes like a hammock," "falls,
not to rise again." The Spirit of God, Who must
have been the real Author of this marvellous prophecy, looks forward from afar—so far that He
is not concerned to discriminate carefully the intervening periods; but follows the earth in its present condition to its very end. But never must one
prophecy of Scripture be interpreted alone; throw
the light of others upon it, and we know that before
that finality, Jesus must reign one thousand years.
For this in v. 21 the prophet goes back to the hour
of divine intervention when Jehovah shall punish
the host of the high ones that are on high, and the

kings of the earth upon the earth. Who *can* these high ones on high, who are distinct from the high ones of earth, be? There is not the possibility of a doubt or question—they are the angels, or wicked spirits who have, with Satan at their head, revolted from their loyalty to their Creator. Now, like prisoners captured in war, who are temporarily consigned to a pit whence escape is impossible till their final fate is determined, these are consigned to the Abyss; and after many days—at least one thousand years as Revelation tells us—they shall be visited. This follows the rebellious hosts to their end; and then again the Spirit goes back to speak of the reign of "Jehovah of Hosts in Mount Zion, and in Jerusalem, and before His ancients gloriously."

What a marvellous beam of light we have here, and who amongst those who scoff at the personality of the Devil have ever even considered it? It is the denial, not the assertion of that personality, that is due to crass dark ignorance. The harmony, the grandeur, the consistency of this awful fact with present conditions; the impossibility of those conditions being eternal, and the worthiness of God of such an end, all mark the Word as divine.

The word Abyss is one of that group of words used in Scripture to designate some aspect of the unseen world, or sphere of the dead; such as Sheol, Hades, Pit, Lower Parts of the Earth, Heart of the Earth. Some affix to it a meaning of the utmost precision and definiteness of locality, being assured that it is in the very centre of this globe. But leaving this as introducing a subject that would necessarily involve an examination of each word, and possibly introduce an element of controversy it were well to avoid, there can be no reasonable question but that there are weighty *moral* ideas connected with these terms, far more in accord with the purpose of a divine revelation, and far more important for us to grasp, than literal or physical location. The word Abyss speaks clearly of profound depth; and if we consider God as the Most High—the climax of all that is blessed in Light and Love, Joy and Rest—Abyss would speak of the furthest distance from Him, and the opposite of these.

The very constitution of our beings may necessitate this form of speech that appeals to our senses. It may be the only way, imperfect indeed, for we now only "see through a glass *darkly*," or *"in an enigma"*—yet the only way of bringing to our minds those scenes which are in an entirely different sphere. When an apostle was caught away into Paradise, he heard words that were *unutterable,* as well as not *permissible* to be uttered, when restored to this earth. Thus "up" and "down" have weightier truth embodied in them than literal direction: nearness to God on the one hand, and degradation, or loss of moral dignity, on the other.

The Abyss then is the prison of the Devil, his

hosts of high ones, and kings of the earth during the time of the reign of man in the Person of the Lord Jesus over the earth. He is during this time hidden from us; we know nothing further of him during this one thousand years, which we assume to be a literal period of time of that length; but it may possibly be a symbolic number. There we must leave him suffering the fulfilment of Is. xxiv: 21, for during this time he shall whisper no evil suggestion into the ear of any easily deceived Eve; nor bring to death any easily led Adam. Whatever evil may be in the earth shall be quite apart from his immediate allurements.

But we have not come to his final condition yet, nor has this poor earth yet reached its *rest*. It is the 6th day; and in it, as of old, The Man and His Bride shall reign. The seventh follows, the sabbath of eternity.

CHAPTER XXVI.

Satan Loosed from Prison.

Contents.

The thousand years come to their end at last. It has been a time of wondrous blessedness

"Foretold by prophets and by poets sung
Whose fire was kindled at the prophet's lamp."

The earth has basked in the beams of the Sun of Righteousness and over all its fair extent, the knowledge of the Lord has covered it with joy and happiness, even as the wavelets of the sea sparkle and dance in the summer sunshine and cover all beneath them. But not even yet is unmixed perfection reached; so it must end, and Satan has one more service to perform, ere he is consigned to his last long home. Once more shall he test and try mankind; to show if anything other than sovereign grace can really change man in the flesh, or win man's wretched heart to God.

SATAN.

Unchanged himself—no penitence, no humbling have a thousand years of prison worked; but he is loosed, and over earth's fair fields he takes his flight, marks the peace and happiness that flood its scenes; sees his erstwhile kingdom under its rightful King, The Son of Man; no dark places are there now, the abodes of cruelty; no shameful evils done in secret; no antipathies even among the beasts; no strife either in insect or vegetable world; all is in its pristine paradisiacal harmony and beauty.

Is all as fair as it seems? Has one thousand years of perfect government served to give a new life, a new heart, a new birth to every man? Alas, that it must be written, the event proves but too surely that that which "is born of the flesh is flesh" and nothing else, and Satan succeeds once more in deceiving the nations of the earth.

I am indebted to another * for the suggestion that there may be a real significance in the term "four *corners* of the earth." It suggests remoteness from the centre Jerusalem; as if, as the years sped on through that happy time, there had been an almost natural instinctive gravitation away from the Seat of that Government of Light, on the part of many. So that upon his return, the Devil finds those who have thus gravitated away to those distant parts "the four corners," only too ready to listen to his deceptive words.

*Numerical Bible by F. W. Grant.

LOOSED FROM PRISON.

But two strange words are added: "Gog and Magog"—What is their significance? They point to the source whence the hostile companies, amongst whom the Devil is successful, come. Not one soul *in Israel* is deceived; all are from *the Gentiles;* and this again harmonizes with the thought derived from the "Corners" of the earth.

Magog was the second son of Japheth, whilst Gog is the name given to the leader of the hosts against the "unwalled villages" (Ez. xxxviii:11) and is said to be "of the land of Magog."

The meaning of the word "Gog" may also throw its light on the passage. It is akin to *Gahg* "top," "roof" and to point in Ezekiel to the lofty dignity of him who bears the title—for it is thought to be an official, rather than personal name, cognate with *kak, khan.** Whilst it may well have here a strong suggestion of the *moral* character, of him or them of whom it speaks—telling us of the same awful sin that was the first, and is thus seen to be the last: lofty pride, "Gog denotes him who sets himself like a *roof* in the midst between heaven and earth."

It would appear then that, as all through the ages of time, history shall once more repeat itself, and the final attack on the land of Israel, as described in Ezek. xxxviii-xxxix, when their last enemy the Assyrian is destroyed, furnishes a type

---

*A traveller calls a Tartaric chief of the 13th century *Gog Khan.* (From Lange.)

of this the last attack of all the powers of evil on all that is of God in this earth.

It has been thought by some indeed that we have here exactly the same time, and the same occurrence as in Ezekiel, but this would hardly appear tenable from the words of ch. xxxviii:17, *"Art thou he of whom I have spoken in old time by my servants the prophets of Israel, who prophesied in those days (many) years, that I would bring thee against them."* And again, ch. xxxix:22, *"So the house of Israel shall know that I am the Lord their God from that day and forward."* Now Israel, without a question, learns that Jehovah is indeed her God, *before,* and not after the millennial reign of her Messiah—of that there can be no question—whilst her prophets have constantly foretold an attack on the part of "The Assyrian" that should be the last chastening from her Lord; for in the destruction of this Assyrian His indignation with His people Israel should cease forever (Is. x:25).

The scenes being confessedly so remote may well account for our difficulty in discovering details; but it would appear that the words "Gog and Magog" are added here; first to suggest to us the lofty proud spirit that still characterizes or governs these hordes of deceived men; their nature is the same as his who comes to deceive them. Secondly, that the terms include all those who are really Gentiles for as he is not a *Jew* who is one outwardly,

neither is he a Gentile who is one outwardly, for
in both cases are there moral significances in the
term used; and Gog and Magog are used here to
include all who are Gentiles in that deeper moral
sense of *not knowing God* as 1 Thess. iv:5 clearly
speaks. This history of earth's nations thus ends
here, as it began in Gen. x and xi, in pride and
judgment. As sea-sands in number men again
revolt against God and His Christ. "Flesh," enmity
against God to the very end, even welcomes—oh,
sad that it must be said!—the deceptions of the enemy, always and in all places. Indeed to-day one can
see exactly the same thing in the way deceptions,
that destroy every hope, are welcomed. One would
suppose that if we had been *compelled* to believe
that there were no Creator of all, or that He was
not interested in His creation, or that He had not
given His Son to put away the sin that is surely
not to be denied; it would be with bitterest sorrow,
and many tears. Alas, men welcome these mur-
derous lies, as if they involved blessedness. But
dreadful as this is, it at least *confirms* the truth of
all it denies. Soon organized are the forces of evil,
and if the proud unregenerates have gravitated
away from the centre of light, the humble saints
have gravitated to it, so that the Beloved City is
the centre of attack. We are quite unable to see
any other city than Jerusalem here, no longer called
Sodom, but *beloved*. But round about the city is
an encampment of saints—may these not be *pious*

Gentiles, who have also drawn near to the divine attraction of the royal city?

There is no fighting. Heaven is too close to earth in these days, the inter-communion too near and quick for the enemy to have any success, even temporary. Fire comes down out of heaven from God and devours the armies of the Devil.

As to that wonderful being whose character and career we have endeavored to trace: he is cast into the Lake of Fire, not to reign there; but beneath the lowest depth of misery, degradation, and wretchedness, for eternity; in hell at last and forever, it is his endless end!

And now, for the last time, Christ's Judgment Seat is set. We have already seen it in heaven, following the casting out of Satan thence, with saved saints only manifested before it. Then on earth, following Satan cast out thence, with both saints and sinners discerned in its holy light. Now, Satan being cast out of both heaven and earth, for the third time that awful Seat is set, and before it stand none but impenitent sinners of the human race; who share the awful sentence of their Deceiver, the Lake of Fire. Thus in his Person, Work, Place, and Destiny there is harmony from the beginning of the Scripture to the end; and all the books that have reference to him show such a unity of design as compels the conscience and reason to see, not a variety of human writers, but one divine Author behind them all.

LOOSED FROM PRISON.

From the very first glimpse we have of him to the very last, there is no such thing as a correction or rejection by later writers of what has preceded. No lengthened period elapses in our day without a thorough rejection of very much that had previously been considered settled, but the Devil cast into the Lake of Fire is indeed far more revealed, his evil has developed, the veil about him has been dropped, the pretension to being solely governed by a zeal for righteousness is no longer made, he stands before us, *naked,* as it were; but he is still not the pitiful, petty, contemptible being that modern folly, pride, and ignorance love to imagine him; and, based on that imagination, reject. He is stupendous to the end: the mighty leader of mighty hosts of evil.

Gradually has he been manifested. At first hidden altogether behind the serpent, we should have known nothing of him but for later writings; then we get glimpses of him ever and anon, always protesting Godward against the unrighteousness of pardoning guilt; and manward against the unrighteousness of the divine dealings—so separating, always, between God and men. Then the Son of God comes on the scene, and in His Light the Devil, as all else, is fully exposed, till he casts out the Heir, kills Him, and has the inheritance of the earth for himself. The marvel is that this is permitted, as it still is; but we see, in the Church, a reason worthy of God for the permission, and one that

He only could conceive. The Devil dwells in, and reigns over the earth still, and will till the number of the heavenly elect shall be completed; then comes that happy morn of morns when we shall all be, with one joyous exultant rising, with the Lord; and the Devil shall have no more place in heaven, where he has still access to accuse us day and night. A 1,000 years in the abyss, a shorter release, and eternity in the Lake of Fire closes his history. But there is a perfect unity in that history, that would have been absolutely impossible, if merely the work of human authors, separated by the strongly varying environments of 1,500 years or more.

Reject the personality of Satan, or the Devil, and what follows? Not only are we left without any worthy explanation of that most undeniable phenomenon: sin; and the strange mixed condition of things in the earth; but we have really lost all revelation. For he is not only clearly revealed, but his being is in the very warp and woof of Scripture —it cannot be torn out without tearing to shreds, and ruining the whole fabric. Christ, the Son of God, as we have seen,* is lost; and, with Him, His God and Father is lost—all is lost! The denial of the personality of Satan is but the thin edge of the wedge that shall rive the soul from all divine revelation.

---

*Page 5.

CHAPTER XXVII.

THE LAKE OF FIRE.

Contents.

Thus we come to consider, as far as it has pleased God to tell us of it in His holy word, and as He in His grace permits, that awe-inspiring term "the Lake of Fire." As the eternal abode of the lost— whether rebel spirits, or the finally impenitent of our fellowmen—it surely cannot but be of the profoundest and most solemn interest to seek for such light as His word affords.

The term itself occurs in the Book of Revelation only, and six times, all in the closing chapters. The first who are said to be cast into it are "the beast and false prophet," who, without passing through natural death, are consigned to its torments, *alive*.

Thus it would appear as if two rebellious impenitent men preceded even the Devil into that Fire that was alone prepared for him.

SATAN.

Nor do the terms of Scripture permit us to think of the existence of these human beings as extinguished by that Fire, for after the one thousand years of Messiah's reign on earth, they are still said to be there, and not only in existence, but conscious; for they are to be "tormented day and night for ever and ever."

The Fire then does not have the same effect as would natural fire upon man's being. Is it natural fire at all? This has been, and is, so strongly contended for in some quarters, as if any question with regard to it were akin to simple infidelity, that one is bound to consider it carefully.

God has created everything with which our senses make us familiar with a far deeper purpose than merely their recognition by those senses. These are but the external court; for their real meaning one must enter the Sanctuary itself; let the divine light that shine there teach us. All nature is a book of parables. From sun, moon, and stars, down to the smallest creeping thing, all have a voice to an ear that is opened to hear, and all witness to invisible, spiritual, eternal verities. Our blessed Saviour, in the days of His sojourn here, dealt much with this book, and taught most precious lessons from it.

Thus we are at least not unprepared to entertain the thought that natural fire, standing for something *not* literally that, has been made, in order to bring to our minds, in a way not otherwise possible, the truth of that unseen world. Thus that truth is not affected at all, nor weakened in the slightest degree, by the recognition that we are dealing with symbols and figures, and not with mere natural phenomena.

And this is really necessitated by another consideration. When the Lord plainly told us that the fire into which the "cursed" amongst men would be consigned had been *"prepared for the Devil and his angels,"* He gave us at least two truths to consider: 1st, that it was not the prime intent and purpose of God (blessed be His Name) for *men* to be consigned there at all; 2nd, that the fire was not of the ordinary character "prepared" for the service of men, and which has effect on matter; but quite distinct from this, since it is specially "prepared" for and having effect upon, *spirits.* This really should be enough to settle the question permanently nor should any hesitate as to accepting this, for only thus do they honor the Lord's own word, and this can never be other than safe.

So in the Old Testament, God has, in Israel, in many marvellous and interesting ways, both in the history of the people, and even in the topography of the land, given us pictures or types of unseen and eternal truths; but the types must not be confounded with what they typify.

Thus *Ge-Henna,* the strict "Hell" as the place of final punishment is, when translated, the "Valley of Hinnom," which was outside Jerusalem, where the material filth of the city was burned. It was the "draught," the receptacle for the sewage of the city.

The Lord's use of the word Gehenna, or Hell, in Mark ix, points clearly to the last verse of Isaiah. *"And they shall go forth and look upon the carcases of the men that have transgressed against me; for their worm shall not die, neither shall their fire be quenched; and they shall be an abhorring to all flesh"* (Is. lxvi:24).

Here, as always in such cases in the Old Testament, all is literal and material: carcase, worm, fire, but all, too, are figures of what are not material or literal. The carcase that tells of the first death is a picture, not of the first, but of the second. The worm in the heap of filth was a figure of the internal gnawing of conscience all alive and awake and never to slumber more, never dulled, never silenced, never seared: *"their"* worm (each one having his own) dieth not." The fire, too, is a figure of the eternal suffering from the wrath of God, and there is nothing that can extinguish this fire; it is eternal. Thus is the word for wrath constantly used in Scripture; and, quite consistently with this, we again and again read of wrath "waxing hot"; "wrath kindling"; "wrath consuming," etc.; it as a *fire,* and is so figured.

So, when our Lord, evidently referring to this verse in Isaiah, counselled man to cut off hand, or foot, or to pluck out an eye, He did not mean that men should thus literally mutilate their bodies. These outward members, like the "lip" (Is. vi), or "tongue" (James iii), only represent the nature or *will* behind them, and which they serve.

THE LAKE OF FIRE.

But this being beyond all controversy the case, it follows, necessarily, that both "worm" and "fire" are equally figurative; nor, as previously said, is their force weakened in the slightest degree by this truth. The thing figured answers absolutely to that which figures it, only in another sphere—whilst this discrimination is of great importance in aiding us to a scriptural view of this most solemn theme.

Thus the Fire in the Lake of Fire is that awful Wrath that God never intended to visit on men (Matt. xxv), and was borne as Judgment by His beloved Son, during the last dark three hours on the Cross, where the literal fire that consumed the sin-offering of old, found its antitype in this consuming judgment of God; but it was "prepared" before man was called into being, for the Devil and his angels.

Surely not one of my readers would deny that our blessed Lord bore man's twofold appointment, Death and Judgment (Heb. ix:27); not indeed in the order of first the Death, and *after that* the Judgment; but, that we might be well assured that both had been borne, He suffered the Judgment *before* the Death; but who would contend that that Judgment was, or resulted in, literal fire? But if this is man's final appointment, how could it be anything else? This should be absolutely conclusive.

Why a Lake? The idea in the word is repression, confinement; and, like that Dead Sea, that seems so strangely, yet perfectly to figure it, *there is no outlet!* The river of Death (Jordan) flows steadily into it; but there is no outlet. Evil is there, ever there, unchanged, but limited, confined, repressed on every side by One who now intervenes and says, "No Further" (Job. xxxviii:2). No Throne is there. The Devil does not reign; but as he falls from a greater height, so does he sink to a lower depth of shame and suffering than any other creature.

So the Word of God, throwing its holy light far into the future, even into eternity, shows us that things shall never be—alas!—as they were prior to evil being found in God's creation. But why say "alas"? It is true that God never simply restores as before, but then does He leave things *worse* than they were, or better? Always better. But before evil was found in Satan, all was "very good," as in this Adamic creation before sin had marred it; whilst even in the eternal scene, in one spot at least, there is evil still—"weeping, wailing, gnashing of teeth"—"beast," "false prophet," "Satan," his angels, and soon everyone not found written in "the book of life" are in the Lake of Fire. Is then the Lake of Fire an improvement on the original creation, as it came from God's Hand? In that Lake all the evil of all creation—all the moral sewage of the universe is gathered together, as, in the smaller scale, the material sewage was in Tophet, in the Valley of Hinnom. Were it not better to blot it out altogether, and leave nothing to evidence, or hold in memory the wrongs and sorrows of the long ages of sin's existence and activity?

The very fact that it is not blotted out is proof enough for childlike faith that it would not be better; or He who does all things well, would, had it indeed been possible, have so ordered it. The mere extinction of evil would not permit its rendering its tribute to His glory. Evil has ever done this; ever has the eater—not been extinguished, but—been made to yield meat, the strong sweetness (Judges xv), and is not *that,* at least, far better?

No, the Lake of Fire is the necessary witness to God, that completes, or perfects, that scene of universal bliss that follows for eternity. It keeps, not merely evil in memory, but that side of God's holy nature that otherwise would have no expression in that scene of blessedness. All else speaks of the *goodness,* this of the *severity* of God, and *this, too,* is a part of His glory—for even where mercy is rejected, God can still make the impenitent to show forth His glory; and even the subject of our consideration, the Devil, shall in this way at least justify his creation.

There is then a sense in which the eternal existence of that scene of active wrath, and of repressed evil, the Lake of Fire, is not worse than the primal creation that spoke only of His *goodness,* but left entirely unanswered the question of how would it be if His Will were opposed, and evil introduced? Would it overcome Him? Or would He be reduced to show power alone and annihilate it? It comes, and eternity tells out the story of His dealing with it: how it has permitted God to express Himself in His perfection. He loved. He *so* loved as to give His Son. He thus found a way in unapproachable wisdom to maintain His creation, though sin-defiled; to preserve His relation, nay, strengthen His relation, with His beloved race of men, and yet not sacrifice His holiness. And after all is over, we have a song never heard in the primal creation, a *new* song of sinners saved and redeemed by the death of His Son—there can be no doubt as to *this* being "far better."

But these happy singers belong to a race of creatures with a faculty not to be *compelled* like the inanimate creation, nor like the brutes that are *driven;* they must not be simply forced, but left free; and if some of them reject the only possible way of salvation, and pass out of the scene— lepers still—what can be done to justify their existence, but for them to be witnesses to eternity of the absolute righteousness—the burning holiness of God?

Thus is he, once Lucifer or the Bright Morning Star, now the Devil, Satan, the Dragon, the old Serpent, Beelzebub, Apollyon, Leviathan, Abaddon, made to justify his creation and existence, as his type Pharaoh of old, by being a witness, an eternal witness to the power, holiness, severity of

THE LAKE OF FIRE.

God—even *his* knee bowing; even *his* tongue joining in the universal confession that Jesus Christ is Lord to the glory of God the Father. All shall fully justify His ways in eternity; although now we do, indeed, see through a glass darkly.

CHAPTER XXVIII.

THE ETERNITY OF FINAL RETRIBUTION.

Contents.

Eternal punishment of the impenitent based on the nature of man's being—not an evolved brute—in quite another kingdom—immortality of the spirit—the inequalities of present scene—not righted here—must be elsewhere.—Two-fold character of judgment.—The "harvest" and the "leper"—many and few stripes consistent with eternity of punishment.—Eternal conditions always looked at from *divine* standpoint.—Infinite suffering impossible to any creature—Dependence, the lesson of the ages.—Appeal.

The eternal condition of the Devil is so linked with those of Adam's race who share his crime, his nature, and his lot, that it lies almost in the direct line of our subject to glance at this most solemn—nay, awful theme, of the eternal character of the punishment of the lost; and I propose to consider it, not as a question of revelation—for of that there can be no question—but rather as to the reasonableness of what is revealed.

The root of the matter, from such a standpoint, lies in the constitution of man's being. Is there in him something not in any other visible creature in earth, or air, or sea? Is he, as Science (?) assures us, simply an evolved *brute,* which, in its turn, is an evolved *vegetable,* and that an evolved *clod,* and that an evolved *atom,* and that an evolved—something we know nothing about? Is his being of the same kind exactly as that of his dog or his horse, differing only in *degree* of development? We conceive that truest reason utterly rejects this and bows, in absolute submission to, and harmonious acknowledgment of the clear teaching of Scripture, that places man in another kingdom altogether. Connected with the mineral by his body, with the animal by his soul, he is linked with the divine by his spirit. He is thus, as no beast ever was, the "offspring" of God. Inferior in many respects to many of the animal creation, there is not one that he does not dominate. He is puny and weak, even in his noblest and strongest, compared with the huge and mighty creatures of desert, jungle, or sea; he is short-sighted compared with many of the inhabitants of earth and air; he is beaten ignominiously by many in speed; in keenness of scent he is far behind his own dog; in instinct he is beaten out of all competition. Yet does he, the inferior, put his foot as king, on the neck of all others. Why? Because of him alone is it written, *"God breathed into his nostrils the breath of life,"* and with that breath there was communicated an element, a faculty, that no beast ever had; a spirit, with powers of reasoning, of recognizing and answering to God, that makes him what no beast is, a morally responsible creature, having to account to his Creator for the use made of the life conferred. So speaks the divine Word, for *"everyone of us shall give account of himself to God"* (Rom. xiv:12) ; and simple pure reason adds its Amen to the truth.

But when does he so give account? Now, in this life? Surely the wisest of men was only voicing the perplexity of every thoughtful man who ever lived, when he, looking upon this disordered scene, and noting its inequalities and injustices that were never righted here, cried, *"There is a vanity that is done upon the earth; that there be just men to whom it happeneth according to the work of the wicked; again there be wicked to whom it happeneth according to the work of the righteous"* (viii:14). The very equal lot of death being an inequality since it comes without the slightest discrimination to all alike (Ecc. ix:2, 3).

No, there is no perfectly just retribution here— there is no evidence of a perfect moral government here. Its lack—the clear denial of it, on every hand, has caused the utmost perplexity all through the ages to those who still know well that behind, and above all, there ever is One all-wise, all-mighty, all-good Creator and God; till, even apart from revelation altogether, simple reason has concluded that, as things now are, at least, another scene and sphere must witness the harvest of this earth's sowings, and counselled, *"Rejoice, oh, young man, in thy youth; but know that for all these things God will bring thee into judgment."*

ETERNITY OF FINAL RETRIBUTION.

But nothing, outside of revelation, can go further than this: *"God shall bring every work into judgment"*; but who can overestimate the need of revelation in such a case? We are absolutely dependent for our knowledge of what takes place beyond death on the only One who knows. Our own *knowledge* must be confined to this scene; deduction forces us to discern a future judgment seat, but that is all.

Nor can we expect much light from the Old Testament. Many make a grave mistake here, and quote the ignorance and darkness as therein so often expressed, as being the measure of what has even up to this day been revealed to *us*. To such the coming of the Son of God has had no effect; nor is there much meaning in the words, "Life and incorruptibility have been brought to light through the Gospel" (2 Tim. i:10). To these expositors who can easily minimize the value of the Old Testament on occasion, "life and immortality" are dealt with in equal power and intelligence by David as by Paul, by Solomon as by the Lord Jesus, who is not here at all *"Greater."*

Nay, we may still safely assert that life and immortality were not brought to light even when the last word of the last book of the Old Testament was written. The whole race of mankind is made to await in a longing expectancy—where there is not a moral stupor or death—the coming of One and the only One who does, or can, bring life and immortality to light. God be thanked. He *has*.

So when such texts as Job x:20-22, Ecc. iii:18-21, ix:6, etc., etc., are used as proof texts for annihilation or mortality of man's spirit, or utter unconsciousness after death, it is evident that they are violently wrested from their setting, and their meaning and force distorted. *They express human ignorance;* the limit of human knowledge as far as experience goes; and surely what the wisest or best of men do *not* know, whilst of deepest interest and value to us, and justifying the place in the inspired volume, as showing us the limitations of unaided human reason, and the crying need for another Voice to be heard, yet to make it the limit of divine revelation is as unreasonable as it is dangerous.

We are thus forced to turn to the New Testament, and seek, in the humble dependence that is fitting, to learn what we can as to our subject, and as the same principle already recognized as running all through nature is insisted on in Galatians vi, we may take that as a basis for our further inquiry: *"Be not deceived; God is not mocked; for whatsoever a man soweth, that shall he also reap. For he that soweth to the flesh shall of the flesh reap corruption; but he that soweth to the Spirit shall of the Spirit reap life eternal."*

But if there is to be of every sowing a corresponding reaping, if every word is like a seed that is to result in a future harvest, then surely the future lot of each one must be a *very checkered one.* No one has sown *only* good seed; no one, one would think, had sown bad indiscriminately. How then is such a principle consistent with absolute bliss on the one hand, with one common Lake of Fire on the other?

This question forces us to ask if there be not some other principle of divine judgment as well as that of the harvest? Some principle that necessitates only two abiding places for eternity, such as are so clearly revealed in Scripture? The answer is clear that there is such a principle and a most important one. God necessarily takes account not only of what a man does (which is the principle of the harvest) but of what he *is,* and a man's dwelling must depend primarily on this last, as we shall see.

Most Christians can recognize the distinction between these two as shown in the Epistle to the Romans. Down to chapter v:11, the subject dealt with is, what I have done, the offenses committed. Then the subject turns to the root whence these sins came; the principle of sin within, what I *am.* So to meet the first the Lord Jesus died for our *sins;* to meet the second He was made sin.

Now it is evident that the first thing that must determine the place of anyone for eternity is what they *are* eternally.

There are only two men, as it were, recognized in the Scriptures: "the first" and "last Adam," "the first" and "Second Man." These are exactly contrary one to the other in every way. The first is governed by a nature that is, beneath all veneers, sin-loving, God-hating, enmity with God, "not subject to the law of God nor can be," and every characteristic of evil that can be thought of as opposed to God; in one word he is *"Sin."* The second is exactly the reverse. He is characterized by every trait of good in harmony with God. "He cannot sin because He is born of God." Now one can easily see that here, at least, is one sharp, clear, dividing line. These two men cannot be in the same place forever. The same surroundings would be impossible for both. The first we may confidently affirm would be as much out of place in heaven as the second would be in hell. Each would be so perfectly, absolutely, out of harmony with environment as to evidence that there was still a moral disorder and confusion that certainly could not be an eternal condition, or it would not be of God, for He is not the Author of confusion. Thus each must be "in his own place," and as to this there is no question necessarily of rewards or punishments. It is simply a necessity from the nature of the case; reason demands it as well as Scripture.

The Old Testament, although it has little direct light on the subject, yet gives an abundance of valuable figures or pictures. Amongst these is the *Leper* in Lev. xiii. Here we have a figure of man in the flesh; what he *is,* evidenced indeed by certain symptoms; but he has, in the type, *done* nothing. The question that the priest has to determine is what he *is*, not what he has *done*. He might personally have been morally upright, but if there was a "rising," a "bright spot," a "white hair," he was declared a leper and unclean. Where then was necessarily his place but outside the camp? But there was no punishment meted out to him there; no stripes, no stoning; not a hand was lifted against him; the glances that followed him as he sorrowfully passed to that desolate place were rather filled with pity than reprobation. He was there —necessarily there—because of what he *was,* not because of what he had *done.* His presence in the place where God dwells would have been an anomaly—the same place could not contain God and the manifested leper. If this was the case in that far-off day, most certainly is it a figure of that other day yet to come in which "the tabernacle of God is with men, and He will dwell with them" (Rev. xxi) in a far wider, truer sense even than in Israel, for then it will not be a question of externals, but of realities, and once more then must every leper be put outside that dwelling of God. He will not, He cannot dwell in a place so defiled. But *"outside"* in that day will be outside the whole scene of blessedness.

Thus, then, the possession of *life,* divine life in the Second Man, alone fits for the dwelling with the living God; this lacking, the second death is the *necessary* abiding place. But life comes only from and with Christ. Hence the one sharp, clear, dividing line between men is their relationship to the Son of God, the Lord Jesus Christ. This determines what they *are;* apart from Christ, they are lepers; but *"he that hath the Son has life,"* *"shall never come into judgment, but is passed from death unto life."* No single one that has Christ, and with Him divine life, can possibly, from the nature of the case, be in the second death; and no single one that passes out of this scene spiritually dead because in separation from God, can, from the nature of the case, dwell in that scene and sphere of Life with the living God.

Thus, speaking plainly, men's eternal dwelling place is determined primarily by what they *are,* not by what they have *done.* But the two principles of judgment cannot be in any way antagonistic to one another. If anyone has Christ, and thus a new divine life, this must necessarily show itself in action, in accord with its own nature. It is *divine,* and hence its display will always have the divine marks of Light and Love. Every thought, every word, every deed, coming from that Life, will be marked by righteousness and love. As the Apostle John says: "He that doeth righteousness is righteous, even as He is righteous," and again, "Every one that loveth is born of God and knoweth God. He that loveth not, knoweth not God, for God is love."

But again—for we have not quite cleared away our difficulties yet—take a man clearly and admittedly **born** of God, yet how often does such—I might say all such—sow to the flesh? Even the "beloved disciple," John himself, could go counter to his Lord—was that flesh or Spirit? Peter could deny Him with oaths—was that flesh or Spirit? Yea, even after being sealed by the Holy Spirit, he could give way in the gravest crisis, and withdraw from the Gentiles, wherein, says Paul, he was to be blamed (Gal. ii)—was that sowing to the flesh or Spirit? Even our own dear Apostle Paul on one occasion could burst out with "God shall smite thee, thou whited wall," and then withdraw the word with sorrow. Surely this was not sowing to the Spirit. And if this the case even with these most honored apostles, what of *us?* And how then can those, who thus again and again sow to the flesh, both "reap" the assured "corruption" that we are told is the harvest of such sowing, and yet, at the same time, enjoy unmingled blessing?

The Word of God gives us a clear answer to this. Even those born of God must be first manifested before the judgment seat of Christ, according to 2 Cor. v:10, which we have already looked at, before they can be manifested in glory with Christ, according to Col. iii:4. It is here the fact that they are true children must be shown out, in that holy, searching divine Light; and the "deeds done" do show it out. For be there but one single word ever spoken that could only have its birth from the divine nature, that word is sufficient to *manifest* the speaker as a true child. And every

239

single saint manifested before that judgment seat must necessarily have that one mark of new birth: *confession of sin and self-judgment*. In this the priestly eye of the Great High Priest sees the healthy "black hair" that always delivers from any suspicion of leprosy (Lev. xiii:37), and pronounces him *clean*. Every act prior to this must necessarily have been a dead work, and as such is burned. Yea, and many an act after it; as, in degree, the honored apostle Peter's at Antioch cannot stand the fire of that day, but is burned, and as far as that work goes he does "reap corruption." Some may and doubtless shall then evidence the truth, of that word, "His works shall be burned, but he himself shall be saved; yet so as by fire" (1 Cor. iii:15). For reaping corruption does not necessarily mean that he is cast into the Lake of Fire. If a man sows tares or thistles, it does not necessarily follow that he is hung or imprisoned for it; but it does necessarily follow that he *reaps* tares. He gets no wheat, no food, nothing of value at all; he suffers loss. There is no escape from that.

Thus, as has been said, these two principles of judgment are not contradictory at all. With the one awful dividing line of Life and Death come an infinity of divergencies or discriminations in the lots of every one on either side of that line— discriminations that are worked out by each individual, as the harvest is the result of sowing.

Now turn to a word of the Lord Jesus that bears most directly on our subject, in Luke xii:47,

ETERNITY OF FINAL RETRIBUTION.

48: *"And that servant which knew his Lord's will and prepared not himself, neither did according to His will, shall be beaten with many stripes. But he that knew not, and did commit things worthy of stripes, shall be beaten with few stripes. For unto whom much is given, of him shall be much required; and to whom men have committed much, of him will they ask the more."*

Clearly retribution is exactly measured by the light enjoyed, and the Lord in speaking of few or many stripes seems to have in mind Deut. xxv:1-3: *"If the wicked man be worthy to be beaten, then the judge shall cause him to lie down, and to be beaten before his face, according to his fault, by a certain number. Forty stripes he may give him, and not exceed; lest if he beat him with many stripes, then thy brother should seem vile unto thee."* It is most interesting to note here God's care even for the wrongdoer—never was he to receive above forty stripes. May we gather from this a principle that God would never give unlimited punishment for a limited fault?

But does not the fact of anything being eternal make it infinite. And how can a *limited* punishment be harmonized at all with *eternal* punishment? The answer is simple: There may be an eternity of time without an infinity of degree. There may be an almost endless series of differences even in twenty years' imprisonment. It may be simple imprisonment with nothing added, or with *"hard labor,"* or with *"one stripe daily,"* "weekly," "month-

241

ly," or "two stripes," and so on; but all exactly the same as to *time*. Thus whilst the abode of the impenitent is equally eternal because the character of each is equally eternal, the degree shall differ in exactly righteous proportion to the *light* rejected, the love turned from.

Mark carefully the Lord's words, No one will be beaten for unavoidable ignorance. He who knew not, is not beaten even with few stripes BE-CAUSE he *knew not;* but because he did things worthy of stripes, *i. e.,* against and contrary to the light he *had,* dim though it was, the light in nature (Rom. i), so that the conscience accuses and affirms the perfect justice of the sentence, there shall be no accusation against divine justice then.

A difficulty still remains, and we must look at it frankly. There are few who have not felt it, even if they have shrunk from expressing it. Let us put it as strongly as possible.

The idea of the "Lake of Fire" is in itself so tremendous, speaks to the mind of such overwhelming suffering, that it would seem folly to talk of any differences of degree in view of this. What matters, comparatively, to one suffering the tortures of *fire,* whether he is at the same time beaten with a few or many stripes? Neither would be felt—swallowed up by the greater suffering. The common suffering of the Lake of Fire thus appears to be so infinitely great as to do away with the possibility of few or many stripes making any difference, *i. e.,* the suffering because of what men *are*—which necessitates the place they are in— is greater than the suffering of penalty for what they have done; and can that be reasonable?

But we must remember that these solemn scenes are looked at entirely from the *divine* standpoint, and therefore the true one indeed. For take the blessedness of the Father's house—of heaven—of being forever with the Lord; would this *be* blessedness to one who hated, feared that Presence and Place above all? From the divine standpoint it is perfect blessedness; and is always so spoken of; from the sinner's it would be perfect misery. How vain and false is the assumed desire of an unrenewed soul for heaven! Put one such there, and instantly, in terror-stricken haste, like the leprous king in the sanctuary (2 Chron. xxvi:20), he would seek an outlet for escape.

So, from the divine standpoint, separation from God, the curse of His wrath and displeasure, the gnawing of conscience, is the highest wretchedness for a creature made to enjoy His love; but from the sinner's standpoint it may still be with all its misery, the only place possible even to be endured. And the degree in which the suffering is felt will correspond exactly with the degree of Light rejected, of Love refused and turned from.

The fire itself—symbol of the wrath of God— will not have the same effect in suffering on all: *"It shall be more tolerable for Tyre and Sidon at the judgment"* than for those rejecting greater privileges. They that know and turn from the fullest expression of love will suffer most from wrath; those that had most light will most suffer from the contrast of outer darkness. If one had absolutely no light (are there any such?), would darkness be felt by him at all? To those born blind night and day are forever alike.

In conclusion, no *man* will, or can, suffer *infinitely*. Punishment must be limited in degree, but all who make or love a lie must be in the place corresponding to that nature as long as the nature is there—as the leper was outside the camp *"all the days of his leprosy."* If there is any well-founded hope of grace working in that scene a change of *nature,* or the introduction of a new nature, then may there be an equally well-founded hope of a change of *place. Scripture gives no such hope anywhere,* as far as I am aware, and surely it would be plain, clear, simple, if there at all.

As to the Devil, Satan, once the highest creature; then shall he be the lowest, most miserable of all. But since he is but a creature, he is therefore finite, and this precludes *infinite* suffering even in his case.

But One is Infinite, capable of enjoying and who ever did enjoy infinite *Light,* to Him the suffering in that awful darkness on Calvary was *infinite* suffering. Capable of enjoying and who ever did enjoy, infinite Love, to Him the suffering, when waves and billows of judgment passed over His blessed Head during the last three hours on the cross, was immeasurable, *infinite* suffering.

But whilst thus *infinite* and affording thus a perfect ransom-price for "whosoever will"—"the whole world"—shall it, can it be *eternal?* Can Divine Judgment be His *abode?* Can He *dwell* in it? Is that *"His Own place?"* Nay, indeed nay. What He *is* must govern this, and He is manifested even here—alone, forsaken—as infinitely perfect. He stands where no creature, be he the highest spiritual Intelligence, ever did or could stand: *alone!* This is the one lesson of the ages for every intelligent creature to learn, that dependence on the Creator alone can maintain him. Angels must learn it first, and the highest of them all—pride taking the place of dependence falls with an awful moral crash. He, untempted by any superior Intelligence, for there were none, shall remain in the place he has also put himself, alone, "forsaken of God;" and yet confined on all sides as are the waters of a lake; reaping as he has sown in the *Lake of Fire* forever and forever.

Man next comes on the scene; and, tempted by the devil, he too forsakes God, and thus he falls; but the Second Man, Jesus, now comes, and standing in the first man's place, is Himself forsaken of God, and is left alone, utterly alone. HE STANDS! He falls not. He, with unaffected holy submission and piety, justifies God even in His extremity with "Thou art holy" (Psalm xxii). Oh, surely, *"three hours"* of infinite suffering suffice to manifest Him fully thus; and judgment must pass, it cannot linger there; the eagles must fly, for there is no carcase

there, and the highest glory is His for eternity—a
glory He shares with all His own who acclaim
Him only "worthy." To Him "be glory for ever
and ever. Amen."

My dear readers, I would speak to each of you
as if we were alone together. Is not all this not
contrary to, but far above the highest unaided human reason, and *therefore* "reasonable" as being
divine? Could any human mind invent such a mar-
velous plan, or human love and power carry it out?
It must be conceived by Him whose thoughts are as
high as the heavens above the earth. Is it unreasonable then that if we turn away from this infinitely tender love, this only Saviour, we, even we,
must necessarily have our part with him whose
proud, independent nature we thus manifest, and
that forever? Oh, may no heart to whom these
words come receive this grace of God *in vain!*

CHAPTER XXIX.

THE SON OF GOD MANIFESTED.

Contents.

But we will close our meditation on this solemn
theme with a happier, sweeter word; and what we
have already dwelt upon may make this both
doubly clear and welcome.

*"For this purpose the Son of God was manifested
that He might destroy the works of the Devil"*
(1 John iii:8).

We have seen that "the works of the Devil" are
by no means limited, at least, or indeed principally,
to those popularly supposed, and that not one
peculiarly depraved class of mankind evidences
those works, but the whole race. They are as
manifest in the palace as in the gutter; on the
magistrate's bench as in the prisoner's dock; in the
pulpit as in the pew. *Wherever there is a human
heart away from God there is the Devil's work.*

SATAN.

But the Son of God has been manifested to undo or to destroy these works of the Devil. If anyone then ever really sees the Son of God—ever finds or discovers Him, then, as far as that one is concerned, the Devil's work is destroyed forever. Do you simply believe that, dear reader? If so I am sure you will join hands with me, and will search until we find this Son of God, nor rest until we do for it will be no vain profitless quest.

Let us begin in the highest heights of heaven— let us peer amid the ranks of spiritual principalities and powers: carefully search amid the serried ranks of angels—we know none—the Son of God is not there—no, for so says the divine word: *"He took not hold on angels."*

Then we must drop to earth and there too we will begin with the highest, for surely no earthly palace can afford a glory equal to the dignity of such an one. To Caesar's courts we will go, and search its marble halls and golden canopies filled with all the grandeur earth can give. In vain— there is not a sign of the presence of the Son of God there; but rather is it filled with every evidence of the enemy.

Perhaps amongst the mansions of the rich and noble and great ones of the earth we may be more successful. No, He is not there.

Let us make trial of the more modest homes that are really more suitable to domestic comfort—let us omit none. Alas, we find Him not, He is not there.

Then lower still we will go, and search the cottages of the poor for He *has been* manifested, and we *must* find Him. Oh, weary, fruitless search, He is not even there.

Yet, be not discouraged; let us go to that inn filled with travellers; but learning by experience, we will avoid now the inn itself, and go at once to the lowliest spot we can find: to those buildings in the rear. We hear the beasts stamping and chewing their food; our nostrils are filled with the odor of the stables and we are inclined to turn away repelled: surely He cannot be here! Nay, look in one of those mangers, and there a lowly Infant lies: by many infallible proofs, it is the Son of God; *we have found Him at last.*

Look well—sinners as we are, we need not flee. That little Hand will not smite us; those little Feet will not spurn us: those Lips will not curse us. Oh, surely, surely, if that dear Babe is really "God manifest in the flesh," the very sight is enough to win the wanderer back in self-abhorrence, and to loosen the Devil's bonds.

But wait, trace His weary way on earth; past holy childhood to holy manhood, and see Him now, amid a throng of penitents who stand on Jordan's banks, and are being baptized confessing their sins. John discerns Him as the Son of God, and humbly says, *"I have need to be baptized of thee, and comest thou to me." "Suffer it to be so now,"* He answers, *"for so it becometh us to fulfill all righteousness"*; and then He goes down in figure unto Death for the sinners amongst whom He has taken His place. At this sight, the very heavens break open under the weight of the divine delight and appreciation that pressed upon them, and God's Voice is heard owning that Man as His *"beloved Son in whom"* He *"is well pleased." We have found Him.*

Follow His path further; it is as well marked as a ray of light amid black darkness. Wherever He goes, sickness, sorrow, death, flee. The Devil has had his way long upon the earth; and its sins, misfortunes, miseries, express his reign. Where Jesus is, God has *His* way, for He goes "about doing good, healing all oppressed of the Devil." As we see the lame to walk, the blind to see, the lepers to be cleansed, and as we listen to words that none but God could speak to poor self-confessed sinners, *"thy sins are forgiven,"* surely, surely, we have found the Son of God at last.

If such a life can have an end, what can that end be? He shall be translated quietly as Enoch, from this filthy scene, back to His own place, and He shall not be found. No, not thus. Then peradventure fiery chariots shall attend Him home as Elijah. No, not thus. Then at the very least, the *peaceful* end of the "perfect" and "upright man" shall be His (Ps. xxxvii:37). Not thus: not even thus. Wait, and prepare for a marvel, that shall make all other marvels commonplace.

Three shameful crosses stand upon the hill outside the Holy City; and upon them hang three men;

all assumed trangressors of the law. You ask the name of him on the left hand? I know it not. Would you know who hangs upon the right! I cannot tell. I only know that both are being executed justly for crimes committed: they *are* transgressors. But if you ask who is it filling that central cross, I know it well, will you believe it? It is the *Son of God*— His only Son—His delight—His Isaac whom He loves! Have we indeed found the Son of God and in *such* a case?

But why does He hang there—cast out of earth; by heaven too cast out—rejected of both? He is the object of all contumely: high and low, rich and poor, religious and profane, all unite in pouring floods of scoffing on His Head. Can *that* be the Son of God?

Human, and particularly religious, malice, the Devil's craft and rage, God's counsels for once are in accord in effect, although each for a far different end, in putting Him there.

But at 12 o'clock the storm of human scoffing ceases: the cloudless sun suddenly, and from no natural causes, shines not: thick darkness envelopes the scene; and absolute silence takes the place of the noisy babble. What is taking place? Oh, surely, another storm is sweeping with its waves and billows over that holy Head; for at length after three hours, the silence is broken, and a cry pierces the darkness, till it strikes a heaven not opened now, but closed even to Him *"Eli, Eli, lama sabacthani."*

SATAN.

Oh, think, my beloved fellow-sinner, fellow-believer, think; on that cross, alone, forsaken, there the Son of God is manifested, and manifested there as bearing our sins—*yours and mine*—in His own Body on the tree. Discover Him there, and the Devil's shackles fall from off our hearts and spirits, and we can but return, as self-abhorred prodigals, who have wandered far, to the God and Father who thus *spared not His own Son* for us.

And were He thus before us would not every form of the Devil's work be negatived? Could we listen to any preacher however gifted, however attractive, however winning, who could cast one shadow of a slur on the intent and efficacy of His holy suffering—on His transcendent Person?

And were He thus before us, His dear path of ever becoming less and less in man's eyes and our own, would be the most welcome to our feet, and we should walk in sweet fellowship with *all* in whom we could discover any trace of likeness to Him—the Son of God.

For were He before us, oh, my beloved brethren all, we should let no minor difference tell the world, by our separation from each other based on it, that it exceeded in value His dear Name—His holy Person: that even His love was not sufficient to bind together those for whom He gave Himself.

Oh God; His Father, our Father; His God, our God, reveal Thy Son *in* us ever more and more—reveal Thy Son *to* us ever clearer, till we cannot see the glitter of earth for the glory of that Light; and we long to be with Him indeed and forever.

But He is there on that Cross no more—it is quite empty now, then we must not stay there, but trace His path still further, and it will be but a re-tracing of the one we took in our search for Him. Past all the cottages, the homes, the palaces, the glories of earth; past principalities and powers of heaven; higher and ever higher, till in the very highest height, on the very Throne of God, we find Him Who was but now in Calvary's darkness and with *our* sins upon Him there. No sins are here, not one taint of their remembrance is upon Him; but He is crowned with glory and honor. Aye, now He is indeed worthily placed as the Son of God. But in all that glory, which may well make us shrink as so inharmonious with our present con-dition, He is still the same Man, with all those marks that tell us that He knows the very worst of us, and has met that worst, by a love so tran-scendent that it requires nothing but His Presence to make even that glory a "place prepared for" us, the Father's House, our own homelike *Home* for-ever.

But one step further; we have left the earth in the Devil's power; shall it so remain? Oh no, He must be manifested, not only to faith, but sight; every eye must see Him (Rev. i:7) ; and, as the Son of Righteousness (Mal. iv:2), shall He throw His healing beams over this fair scene to be made far fairer; for darkness and deathshade; and all the sorrows connected with darkness shall flee, and then shall be "the *restitution of all things which God hath spoken by the mouth of His holy prophets since the world began*" (Acts iii).

And when thus manifested, the sure promise of God is that we shall be manifested with Him (Col. iii), and for that, we must be caught up to Him first (1 Thess. iv:13-16). My reader, of whom I can say, in a lower sense, as being in Christ not having seen I love, keep jealous watch over thine heart, lest rivals come, and the Hope dims, and the upward look changes its direction to earth and droops: till the Hope becomes a cold, formal doctrine held, and loses all its practical power and blessing. Wait—wait on—wait still for only one event, *"His Son from Heaven."* "Oh come, Lord Jesus, come quickly." Amen!